DAY WALKS OF
Canterbury
& Kaikoura

DAY WALKS OF
Canterbury
& Kaikoura

MARK PICKERING

REED

FRONT COVER: The sunlit archway at Dashing Rocks, South Canterbury (56).
BACK COVER: Heathcote towpath looking towards Castle Rock (30).

Disclaimer
Although every effort has been made to ensure the accuracy of information contained in this book, the publisher and author hold no responsibility for any accident or misfortune that may occur during its use. The Department of Conservation (DoC) is continually upgrading and altering tracks. For up-to-date information, DoC should be consulted before attempting any walk.

REED PUBLISHING (NZ) LTD
TE KARUHI TĀ TĀPUI O REED (AOTEAROA)
Established in 1907, Reed is New Zealand's largest
book publisher, with over 600 titles in print.
www.reed.co.nz

Published by Reed Books, a division of Reed Publishing (NZ) Ltd, 39 Rawene Rd, Birkenhead, Auckland. Associated companies, branches and representatives throughout the world.

ISBN-13: 978 0 7900 0945 2
ISBN-10: 0 7900 0945 5

National Library of New Zealand Cataloguing-in-Publication Data
Pickering, Mark, 1953–
Day walks of Canterbury & Kaikoura / Mark Pickering.
ISBN 0-7900-0945-5
1. Hiking–New Zealand–Canterbury–Guidebooks.
2. Canterbury (N.Z.)–Guidebooks. I. Title.
796.5109938–dc 22

First published 2004
Reprinted 2006

Designed by Sally Fullam

Printed in New Zealand

Contents

Inland Canterbury and Arthur's Pass

Christchurch city

Port Hills and Banks Peninsula

South Canterbury

Aoraki/Mt Cook and Mackenzie Country

List of maps

Preface

This guide is intended for both the Kiwi and overseas holidaymaker, as well as local residents who are interested in exploring the diverse and excellent walking areas in Canterbury. It selects the best of the walking opportunities in this large province, presenting the pick of walks from the forests in the high-country foothills, Arthur's Pass National Park, the Port Hills and city walks of Christchurch, the numerous bays of Banks Peninsula, Kaikoura and of course Aoraki/Mount Cook National Park.

In this book you will find information on accessing the start of each day walk, accompanied by a brief description and supplemented with detailed track notes. Points of interest are added to highlight particular characteristics of the area and to describe noteworthy landscape, historical or wildlife features. Approximate travelling times are provided, although these may vary according to the fitness of the party.

Most people will find walks in this book to suit their style; whether it's an afternoon adventure with the kids or a full-on day trip into the mountains.

Mark Pickering

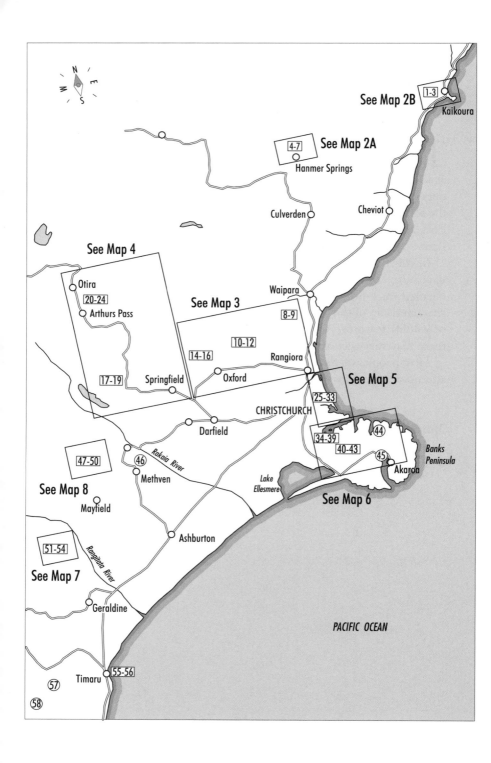

See Map 2B
1-3
Kaikoura

4-7 See Map 2A
Hanmer Springs

Culverden
Cheviot

See Map 4
Otira
20-24
Arthurs Pass

See Map 3
8-9

10-12
14-16
17-19
Springfield
Oxford
Rangiora
Waipara

See Map 5
25-33
CHRISTCHURCH
34-39
44
40-43
45
Akaroa
Banks Peninsula

Darfield

46
Methven

47-50

See Map 8
Mayfield

Rakaia River

Lake Ellesmere

See Map 6

51-54
See Map 7

Rangitata River

Ashburton

Geraldine

PACIFIC OCEAN

55-56
57
Timaru
58

Introduction

Canterbury is one of New Zealand's largest regions and its legal boundaries stretch from the Conway River in the north to the Waitaki River in the south. The boundary runs all the way along the main divide from Lewis Pass to Arthur's Pass, on to Aoraki/Mt Cook and then to Lindis Pass.

This sprawling region is about the same size as the Netherlands, which manages to cram in 15.5 million people, or about 457 people per sq km. In comparison, Canterbury accommodates about 500,000 people, or 30 people per sq km, of which approximately 320,000 live in Christchurch. The spaciousness of Canterbury is one of the region's hallmarks, as well as an extraordinarily diverse landscape.

The Canterbury Plains, one of the largest flat areas in New Zealand, were created by the erosion of gravels from the Southern Alps and are dissected by huge braided rivers, supporting birdlife, such as the wrybill and black stilt, that has adapted to this harsh, shifting environment. Much of the water that drains from the Southern Alps percolates underneath the plains in the form of natural aquifers, providing Christchurch with an enviably high standard of tap water.

Radiating out from the outside rim of the plains are several layers of landscape. At first there is an extensive band of beech-forested foothills, such as are found at Mt Grey/Maukatere, Mt Thomas, Mt Oxford and Mt Somers, all excellent walking areas. Further back, there is a significant sequence of higher mountain ranges, such as the Torlesse Range, with Fog Peak walk (17) going to a height of 1741 m. Part of these foothills includes the Mt Hutt Range, with its famous skifield and a high peak of 2185 m, and Taylor Range behind Mt Somers, with Mt Taylor at 2333 m.

Behind the foothills are large high-country basins of snowgrass tussock, often studded with lakes, such as in the Broken River basin, or at the Ashburton Lakes in the Rangitata Valley. In places the dominant sedimentary rock of Canterbury, greywacke, is broken by rare outcrops of limestone, the best of which can be seen on the Castle Hill walk (18). There are also a number of thermal springs and hot pools in the Canterbury back-country, notably at Hanmer Springs.

Lastly, there are the Southern Alps themselves, and straddling, the main divide, Arthur's Pass National Park is uniquely representative of the

ABOVE: Grasses by the stream in Arthur's Pass (21–24).
RIGHT: Walking on the Port Hills.

high-mountain topography, with beech forest on the Canterbury side and podocarp forest on the West Coast. Arthur's Pass is still an old-fashioned railway village that provides a compact base for walks that take in the waterfalls, beech forest and the high peaks of the area.

The Port Hills are a low dividing range that separates Christchurch from Lyttelton Harbour/Whakaraupo and Banks Peninsula, and are relatively insignificant in the wider landscapes of Canterbury. But to Christchurch people, their distinctive signature skyline and recreational value has made the Port Hills one of the most loved landscapes. Their volcanic origin is obvious if you walk on tracks such as the Crater Rim (36) and around the Sign of the Kiwi (35).

The Canterbury coastline is not as diverse as the mountain landscapes. North Canterbury cliffs and headlands stretch south from the Hurunui River to the Waipara River, with a long stretch of gravel and sand interrupted by river estuaries and lagoons, and on to Christchurch. South of Banks Peninsula, the huge monotonous gravel beach stretching to Timaru used to be called 'Ninety Mile Beach'. At Timaru there is a twist in the coastline at the Dashing Rocks walk (56), then gravel beaches

resume down to the Waitaki River mouth. Kaikoura has a spectacular indented coastline, with rocky coves full of marine wildlife. You can find seals lounging right beside State Highway (SH) 1, and colonies of shags roosting on the rocky promontories. The Kaikoura Peninsula has a wonderful walk and the big tramp up to My Fyffe Hut (2) brings you close-up views of the seaward Kaikoura Mountains.

Banks Peninsula has crammed in all of the coastal scenery that Canterbury lacks, with huge sea-cliffs, gorgeous beaches and numerous deep harbours. The peninsula was originally an island, until the eroded gravel of the Canterbury Plains crept out and finally joined the peninsula to the mainland only 20,000 years ago. The complex hill country of Banks Peninsula has created plenty of walking opportunities on the peninsula, including the tracks through Orton Bradley Park (40–42) and up to the peninsula's highest peak, Mt Herbert/Te Ahu Patiki, or to the Sign of the Packhorse Hut (43).

Lastly, on the far southern edge of Canterbury is the Mackenzie Country, a beautiful upland tussock plain steeped in pioneering history and backed by the big mountains of Aoraki/Mount Cook National Park. Hiking up the Mt John walk (59) is one of the best ways to appreciate this landscape, and if you like your scenery raw the walks that fan out from the Mount Cook village, such as the Hooker Valley (61) and Red Tarn (63) walks, explore one of the most beautiful and harshest parts of New Zealand.

Climate

Canterbury has a mild and dry climate, shielded from the prevailing wet westerlies by the Southern Alps and the foothills. The distinctively warm and dry nor'wester that sweeps over the Canterbury Plains in spring and summer is a föhn wind, and was probably the cause of New Zealand's hottest recorded air temperature of 42.4° at Rangiora on 7 February 1973.

Canterbury also has the record for the heaviest ground frost: -21.6° at Lake Tekapo on 4 August 1938 — and the highest wind gust was on Mt John at 250 km/h on 18 April 1970.

For many Christchurch people, the prevailing summer wind is the 'beastly nor'easterly', a cool coastal breeze that springs up as the land heats up on summer days. Frosts and fog are common in winter with associated smog, but whereas snowfall in Christchurch is rare, the foothills can receive heavy falls that keep the skifields happy (and the farmers unhappy).

Forest and wildlife

It is difficult to appreciate what Canterbury must have looked like before humans settled about 800 years ago. The Canterbury Plains were vast drylands of tussock, cabbage trees and other shrubs, and relatively featureless; it is said that Maori navigated using clumps of prominent cabbage trees. The podocarp forests that you find on the Big Tree (51) and Fern Walk (53) in the Peel Forest of South Canterbury were much more extensive than today, and the same is true of the beech forests around the foothills. Many sawmills in the nineteenth century quickly logged the great 140,000 ha Harewood Forest by Oxford, and similar inroads were made into the podocarp forests of Banks Peninsula, until only tiny reserves remain. Since the 1960s, the spread of second-growth shrub forest on Banks Peninsula has been notable.

Early European pioneers pulled out buried totara logs for firewood in the Mackenzie Country, and the uninterrupted tussock landscape that we see now from places such as the Tekapo Walkway (60) are probably a consequence of human fires and natural environmental changes.

BELOW: Glassy Lake Grasmere, Canterbury high country.

As the forest disappeared, so the bird population declined. Introduced predators such as stoats, weasels and possums have continued the pressure on native birds. The announcement in September 2003 that the orange-fronted parakeet – found only in Canterbury – was facing extinction with a population of just 150 birds, is only a continuation of the sad history of wildlife destruction in the area.

What you can see around Canterbury are all the common native bush birds, piwakawaka (fantail), korimako (bellbird), riroriro (grey warbler), brown creeper and rifleman, with a good chance of seeing the rare karearea (New Zealand falcon) in the high country, and the kea (mountain parrot) at sites like the Temple Basin walk (23) at Arthur's Pass. On the braided riverbeds of the Mackenzie Country you may see the unique wrybill, or the rare black stilt, pulled back from the brink of extinction and one of Canterbury's bird success stories.

Lake Ellesmere is one of the foremost bird sanctuaries in New Zealand with over 160 different species seen here, and it serves as a crucial stopover for migrant wading birds. Christchurch city also has a surprisingly rich diversity of birdlife, with some 20 percent of the world's population of scaup utilising the urban wetlands and rivers at places like Travis Wetland walk (28) and the estuary at Heathcote Towpath (30). Spoonbills are seen in winter months alongside the busy Sumner-to-city causeway.

Maori and European history

Maori arrived in Canterbury about 600–800 years ago, and there were successive waves of tribes who conquered the original occupants, and were in turn conquered. Waitaha, Ngai Mamoe and Ngai Tahu lived semi-nomadic lives, hunting the moa and forming pa around the vast coastal lagoons that occupy all of present-day Christchurch. The estuaries and rivers were full of eel, freshwater crayfish and flounder, and some vestiges of this giant pre-European wetland still remain and can be appreciated on walks to Horseshoe Lake (27) or Brooklands Lagoon Spit (31).

In the summer months, Maori engaged in hunting journeys into the high country, and traces of ancient rock drawings and implements have been found throughout Canterbury. By 200–300 years ago, Maori were crossing the main passes of the Southern Alps regularly either as war parties or in trading groups for pounamu (greenstone).

RIGHT: View from Mt Vernon over Lyttelton Harbour/Whakaraupo.

The last significant Maori war-party leader was Te Rauparaha, from the North Island. Te Rauparaha already possessed muskets when, in 1831, he attacked and overran the Ngai Tahu pa at Kaiapoi – he had already sacked Onawe Pa on Banks Peninsula in 1830. The Maori population was by then considerably reduced by this war as well as by internal feuding and diseases introduced by the early Europeans.

Although some European settlers had already arrived on the 'Port Cooper Plains' (as the Canterbury area was then known) before 1850, it was the arrival of the first four ships to the Canterbury settlement in late-1850 that started the rush of occupations. They arrived at 'Port Victoria' (later Lyttelton Harbour/Whakaraupo) and were faced with the gruelling prospect of getting over the Port Hills and the infamous Bridle Path (39), to the then non-existent city of Christchurch. Modern walkers can retrace the steps of these settlers, well-pleased that they don't have to do that hill in a waistcoat or crinoline! The only remaining example of lowland forest left on the plains can be found at Riccarton Bush (25).

Settlement was rapid and comprehensive across Canterbury, and within thirty years the work of sawmills, back-country burning and establishment of pastoral sheep stations had already created the landscape we are familiar with today. Many day walks in this book step along this pioneering history; for example, following the 1879 Wharfedale Track (15) into the Lees Valley at Mt Oxford, or up the steep incline that leads to the abandoned 1928 Blackburn Coal Mine (47) at Mt Somers.

Walking safety

A few basic tips should keep everyone safe:

- check the weather forecast before going, and adjust plans accordingly
- take adequate clothing, particularly for children
- water, some nibbles to eat and a hot thermos is also useful
- be prepared: some walks require topographical maps, compass and full tramping equipment
- all these tracks and well-signposted and marked. The Department of Conservation (DoC) marks its track with orange triangles
- don't hesitate to turn back if the weather turns foul, or if people are not feeling up to it
- take a cellphone if you wish, but don't expect it to work everywhere

- keep an eye on time, and don't start a major walk in the afternoon. You will be surprised how many Search and Rescue callouts are due to walkers being caught out by darkness
- let someone know where you are going: tell friends or family, use the visitor centre logbook and so on.

Track grades

Please note that these grades are subjective and provided as a guide only. Tracks are given a grade according to their length, gradient and surface.

GRADE 1 Easy
Track surface is well marked, metalled and mostly flat, suitable for children. Approximately 30–40 minutes return.

GRADE 2 Moderate
Track will be clearly marked and well formed, but usually involves some short hill-climbs. Approximately 1–2 hours return.

GRADE 3 Half-day
Track is well marked, may involve some stream crossings, and can be uneven with several short hill-climbs. Approximately 3–4 hours return.

GRADE 4 Fit and full day
Track is well marked, but may be steep with a big hill-climb and go above the bushline. Approximately 5–7 hours return.

New Zealand Environmental Care Code

The saying 'Take only pictures, leave only footprints' is an essential part of everyone's walking equipment these days. The natural environment can only be enjoyed if we look after it.

For some reason people don't seem to count lolly wrappers and paper tissues as litter, but please take all your rubbish home with you. Be pro-active, and remove other people's discarded rubbish.

Please keep to the marked tracks to avoid making the trails too wide, and damaging plants. Lighting fires should be avoided and fire bans observed.

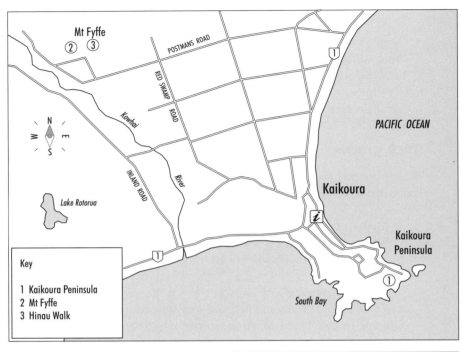

Key

1 Kaikoura Peninsula
2 Mt Fyffe
3 Hinau Walk

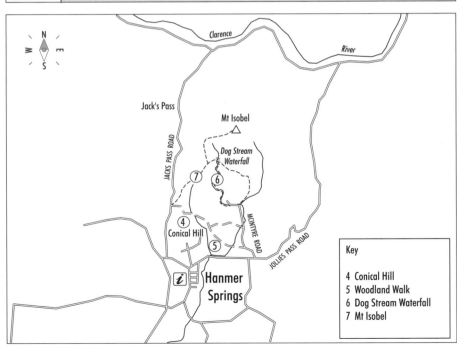

Key

4 Conical Hill
5 Woodland Walk
6 Dog Stream Waterfall
7 Mt Isobel

Kaikoura and Hanmer Springs

Both Kaikoura and Hanmer Springs are popular overnight destinations for Christchurch and Canterbury people, and increasingly for international visitors. At the northern end of the Canterbury region, Kaikoura offers an accessible and dramatic coastline, as well as mountains that come famously close to the seashore. In winter, the white-tipped Seaward Kaikoura Mountains are a dramatic backdrop to the deep blue trench of the Pacific Ocean.

Maori and European settlers came to Kaikoura for the rich marine life, and crayfish (or lobster) are sold up and down the coast. The town has a reputation for some of the best fish and chips in the South Island. Whalemeat and oil are, fortunately, not on the menu these days, but whales have provided an amazing renaissance for the area, turning Kaikoura from a sleepy, fisherfolk town into one of the top tourist destinations in New Zealand.

Hanmer Springs is another town that has grown rapidly, becoming for townies a summer weekend retreat and a ski-resort in winter. 'Forest' in Hanmer means either native beech or pine plantations, the two types mix together with results that are sometimes incongruous and always lovely. Walks are everywhere – the tracks are well maintained and signposted, and this book covers only a few of the better known ones. The forest also has several mountain bike trails, and of course there are the hot pools.

There are good information centres at both Hanmer Springs and Kaikoura, and plenty of accommodation available.

1 Kaikoura Peninsula

GRADE 2

TIME 2–3 hours return on the Shoreline and Clifftop walk circuit via Whalers Bay.

ACCESS From Kaikoura township, drive past the information centre to Point Kean carpark at the far end, where information boards, shelter and a barbecue area are found. Toilets are found 1 km before this carpark. Access can also be gained on the other side of the peninsula, down South Bay Parade to the carpark and recreation area.

ABOVE: Tidal platforms around Kaikoura Peninsula (1).

TRACK NOTES
This walk is best done at low tide, or at least three hours after high tide. From Point Kean, cross the tidal platforms and follow easy shore-trails around to Whalers Bay. Climb up the farm track onto the top of the cliffs and follow grass farm trails back to Point Kean.

POINTS OF INTEREST
- Maori have occupied the peninsula for hundreds of years with over fourteen known pa sites. Kaikoura is a contraction of Te Ahi-kai-koura-a-Tama-ki-te-rangi – The fire at which crayfish were cooked for Tama – a Maori chief.
- European whalers arrived in the 1840s and hunted whales there until the 1920s. Fyffe Cottage (on the road to Point Kean) is an historic whalers cottage and worth a visit. Today, sperm whales and occasionally orca (killer whales), as well as the Dusky dolphin and Hectors dolphin, can be seen in these waters.
- There are striking rock patterns in the extensive tidal platforms and bright limestone cliffs, with many attractive bays and rock pools to explore.

- *Watch out for seals!* They are usually dozing about the shoreline and can be surprisingly hard to spot (though easy to smell).
- *Watch out for dive-bombing gulls!* There are over 12,000 tarapunga or red-billed gulls nesting around the peninsula and they can get pesky at spring with raids on intruders. There are many other shorebirds, including shags and tara or terns.
- Fine cliff-top views over the shoreline and towards the Kaikoura Mountains.

2 Mt Fyffe Hut

GRADE 4

TIME 4–5 hours return to the hut, 6–7 hours return to Mt Fyffe.

ACCESS From Kaikoura township, take Ludstone Road for 8 km to the junction with Postmans Road. Follow the unsealed Postmans Road for 6 km (sometimes the road gets a bit rough) to the carpark. Picnic area and toilets found here.

BELOW: The seat by Mt Fyffe Hut (2) overlooks Kaikoura Peninsula.

TRACK NOTES

There is a broad vehicle track (made in the 1970s) that climbs steadily to the hut, and continues up the tussock ridge to the summit. It's a total distance of 1000 m to the hut, with several seats and a lookout along the way. Take plenty of water.

POINTS OF INTEREST

- The views get steadily better as you climb, and obviously you can return at any point when you think you've had enough. This road is becoming popular with mountain bikers.
- The hut sits snugly on the ridge and is a little oasis after the slog uphill. It has eight bunks and a woodstove, and wonderful views of the Kaikoura Peninsula and the Inland Kaikoura Mountains.
- To continue to the summit and Mt Fyffe (1602 m) itself will take approximately two hours return (500 m climb) from the hut.

3   Hinau Walk

GRADE 1

TIME 40 minutes return.

ACCESS From Kaikoura township, take Ludstone Road for 8 km to the junction with Postmans Road. Follow the unsealed Postmans Road for 6 km to the carpark. Picnic area and toilets found here.

TRACK NOTES

A pleasant family walk through a lovely forest of hinau, kotukutuku (fuchsia), pigeonwood, mahoe (whiteywood) and broadleaf. Good populations of birds including robin, korimako (bellbird), brown creeper and riroriro (grey warbler).

The track starts from the picnic area and meanders through the forest, crossing a small stream at two points, before returning to the exit slightly up from the carpark along Mt Fyffe Road.

POINTS OF INTEREST

- Hinau has white, bell-shaped flowers that make it an attractive garden tree that Maori have many traditional uses for; the bark provides a black dye as well as a pigment for tattooing; a decoction of the bark in a hot bath was reputedly good for curing certain skin diseases; the flesh of the berries made pudding-cakes that were cooked in the hangi. The high tannin content of hinau bark meant that it became an important raw ingredient for the local tanning industry of the nineteenth century.

4 Hanmer Springs: Conical Hill

GRADE 2

TIME One hour return, or by linking with the Majuba Walk and Woodland Walk (5), a two-hour circuit.

ACCESS Hanmer Springs is off SH 7, 130 km from Christchurch. The Hurunui Information Centre is beside the Hanmer hot pools, with information boards and pamphlets available.

TRACK NOTES

Conical Hill (550 m) is something of a 'must do' walk, having an excellent panorama of Hanmer Springs and the mountains beyond at its peak. The track starts from the top end of Conical Hill Road, and is well-signposted. This wide, zig-zag track climbs steadily through the pine forest (note the cafe signposted at the beginning), and past the Majuba Track junction to the round shelter on top. Seats, picnic table and a spot-the-mountain plaque are here.

The Conical Hill track is often linked with the Majuba Walk, which is 20 minutes one-way and leads from the summit down through a somewhat spooky forest of Douglas fir (Oregon pine) to join the Woodland Walk (5). This can be followed back to the town.

Conical Hill, Majuba Track and Woodland Walk combine for a very enjoyable hike, about two hours return from the information centre.

POINTS OF INTEREST

- Early photos of Conical Hill show it covered in tussock and, later, various exotic trees including Lawson's cypress, giant fir, Japanese cypress and Atlas cedar were among the species commonly planted.
- Hanmer Springs is a mix of indigenous beech forest, which is in a conservation park, and an exotic forestry owned by Timberlands (Carter Holt Harvey). There has been considerable effort by locals to secure the more attractive forestry areas as a permanent public resource for walking and recreation.

5 Hanmer Springs Woodland Walk

GRADE 2

TIME 40 minute circuit.

ACCESS The track starts 1 km from the information centre off Jollies Pass Road (on the east side of the roadbridge).

TRACK NOTES

This popular and pretty family walk circuit is signposted beside the roadbridge. The path crosses a footbridge beside Mt Isobel Stream, then turns up the steps, bypassing a charming waterfall before reaching the two ponds. On a calm, clear day Mt Isobel casts a reflection in the ponds.

The track skirts a flax wetland and the junction with the Majuba Track, then crosses over to an impressive stand of redwood conifers. Another turn leads back and overlooks Mt Isobel Stream, completing this little circuit.

The Woodland Walk is all on well-formed trails over gentle, forested country ideal for families and children.

POINTS OF INTEREST

- Many different tree plantings are seen on this route, including Californian and Sierra redwood, and Douglas fir. On Californian redwood trees the bark can be up to 30 cm thick and effectively insulates the trees from fire. The redwoods in Hanmer average 23 m in height – in California specimens have been recorded up to 110 metres!
- Other short walks in this area include Jolliffe Saddle and Timberlands Trail. The *Hanmer Forest Recreation* Department of Conservation pamphlet is very useful for this area, and available from the information centre.

6 Hamner Springs: Dog Stream Waterfall

GRADE 3

TIME Two hours return.

ACCESS After a 7 km drive from the information centre along Jollies Pass Road, turn left into McIntyre Road, and onto Mullans Road to the carpark at the end. More straightforward than it sounds, and signposted, however these roads are sometimes closed for forestry operations.

TRACK NOTES

At first the track is well-graded, and wanders across two footbridges as it goes up the beech-forested valley. However, at the first ford the track changes character, getting noticeably steeper as it zig-zags up alongside the roaring Dog Stream.

At one point the track is cut around a bluff and you get a glimpse of the top of the Dog Stream waterfall. The track then crosses another footbridge and passes the junction with the Spur Track to the top ford.

The last section is short but steep, with a series of staircases that lead you to the elegant waterfall. It is 41 m high as it tumbles over a bluff, and well worth the effort to reach. At this point the altitude above sea-level is 840 m.

POINTS OF INTEREST

- The Link Track that joined the Dog Stream Waterfall track with the Mt Isobel Track has been damaged and is now closed.
- Just before the waterfall, the Spur Track is signposted and this provides a longer round trip for enthusiasts, with a total travel time of 3–4 hours back to Mullans Road.
- A good track for spotting native birds including piwakawaka (fantail), riroriro (grey warbler) and korimako (bellbird) as well as introduced species such as blackbird and song thrush.

7 Hanmer Springs: Mt Isobel

GRADE 4

TIME 5–6 hours return from Clarence Valley Road carpark.

ACCESS From the information centre, follow Jack's Pass Road and then onto the unsealed Clarence Valley Road towards Jack's Pass. After a climb of 2 km, a signposted carpark appears on the right-hand side. **Note:** People also use the alpine route to Mt Isobel from Jack's Pass itself, which is shorter but more exposed.

TRACK NOTES

Because the majority of forest walks are easy, you should not be misled into thinking the track at Mt Isobel is the same. *It is more properly a tramping track, so you should be well-equipped with plenty of food and water.* Mt Isobel is an exposed mountain and snow covered in winter.

The track from the carpark starts in an attractive and unusual setting, passing through groves of elegant European and Japanese larches. Turning up the spur the track enters a sub-alpine scrub belt and passes several seats, before a long sidle across to the top fringe of beech forest. Here the track ascends the main spur through tussock to reach the main ridgeline, and meets the alpine route from Jack's Pass. Follow the well-marked trail as it climbs the various bumps to the high peak of Mt Isobel (1324 m). The views are impressive in every direction.

POINTS OF INTEREST

- From Mt Isobel there are superb views over Hanmer Springs and the remote back country of Molesworth Station, which at 180,000 ha is New Zealand's largest (government run) sheep and cattle farm. The station amalgamated four runs between 1938 and 1949: Molesworth, Tarndale, Dillons and St Helens.
- Once above the bushline you can sometimes see the karearea (New Zealand falcon). Their call is a mewling, squeaky 'kek kek' in flight.

Foothills Forests

The foothills forests in North Canterbury run in an arc from Mt Grey/ Mautakere at the eastern end around to Mt Oxford by the Waimakariri River gorge. They offer many excellent short and long walking tracks, and a climb to any one of these summits on a good day will reward you with tremendous views across the Canterbury Plains. There's plenty of choice for family groups or the fit walker.

Most of the main access roads have pleasant picnic areas, some have camping, and tracks are well signposted. Even in Canterbury's famous nor'westers, these forests are often sheltered and do not receive anything like the rainfall of the Southern Alps.

Most of the forest is beech forest with scattered podocarps such as rimu and kahikatea, and there is usually a healthy population of birds. Exotic forestry plantations often lie on the boundaries of these conservation parks. Wasps feed on the honey-dew in the beech forests, and can be problem in the late summer and Easter periods.

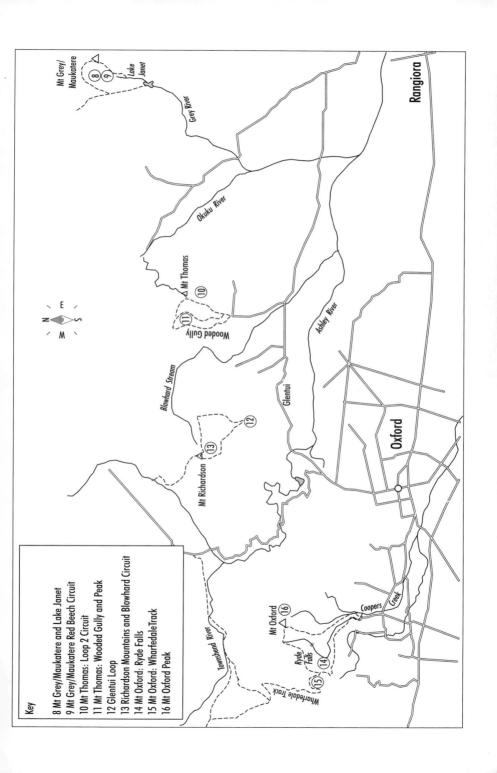

Key

8 Mt Grey/Maukatere and Lake Janet
9 Mt Grey/Maukatere Red Beech Circuit
10 Mt Thomas: Loop 2 Circuit
11 Mt Thomas: Wooded Gully and Peak
12 Glentui Loop
13 Richardson Mountains and Blowhard Circuit
14 Mt Oxford: Ryde Falls
15 Mt Oxford: Wharfedale Track
16 Mt Oxford Peak

ABOVE: Beacon at the very top of Mt Grey/Maukatere (8).

8   Mt Grey/Maukatere and Lake Janet

GRADE 3

TIME 2–3 hours return to Mt Grey/Maukatere from Lake Janet.

ACCESS From the town of Amberley on SH 1, follow the Douglas Road, then Baker Road on to Cramptons Bush Road. At this junction a signpost will warn you if logging operations have closed the main access road. It is an easy drive through the pine plantation to Lake Janet.

TRACK NOTES

From Lake Janet, a good track climbs steadily to the fire lookout through pine trees and broom (which can overgrow the track), and then follows a ridge track and vehicle road up to a transmitter mast.

It is then a short climb over easy tussocks to the beaconed summit of Mt Grey/Maukatere (934 m) itself. It is better to return the same way, as the access road wriggles along an overly long descent.

POINTS OF INTEREST

- The tiny Lake Janet was named after Janet Black who, with her husband Robert, visited the lake often in the 1880s. It is a serene spot with picnic tables, a lookout, native bush and English trees (established by Robert Black), and a good view back over the plains. There is a five minute walk around the lake, and it always seems to have a large and vocal bird population.

- Maukatere means 'floating mountain', so-named because Maori believe the spirits of their ancestors left from the summit on the long journey towards Cape Reinga (literally, the leaping place).
- The peak today is named after Sir George Grey, governor and premier of New Zealand from 1845–79. Because Mt Grey/Maukatere is at the end of the Canterbury foothills, it is a prominent peak and can be seen widely from Christchurch and North Canterbury.

9 Mt Grey/Maukatere Red Beech Circuit

GRADE 3

TIME 6–7 hours return for full circuit.

ACCESS Follow the directions as for (8) to Lake Janet, then continue down the unsealed road through the pine forest to the Grey River/Mawheranui and picnic area.

TRACK NOTES

This is a strenuous circuit up one spur of Mt Grey/Maukatere and down another. Good views are to be had from the summit and the track is generally well marked, but it is a long way so do not underestimate it.

From the carpark, cross the ford and follow the smoothly graded Mt Grey/Maukatere track as it climbs through the beech forest and passes a short side-track to the Gorge Pools. The main track continues in numerous zig-zags up to a lookout track junction.

A tad further is the Bypass Track to Lake Janet, while the main track reaches an open spur with wide-ranging views and then winds its way right to the beacon and summit of Mt Grey/Maukatere.

For those who wish to complete the circuit, follow the poled route from the summit on the open spur to the stile at the bushline. This is now the Red Beech Track, and although well marked it takes a long time down this beech spur, through occasional clearings, to get to the Grey River/Mawheranui.

With some jumping you might be able to avoid wet feet at this crossing. Then the track wanders amiably beside the Grey River/Mawheranui for about two hours until you arrive back at the picnic area.

ABOVE: Summit slopes of Mt Grey/Maukatere overlooking Red Beech Stream (9).

POINTS OF INTEREST

- Beech forest dominates, but there good examples of podocarps, including kahikatea, matai and rimu, particularly in the lowland areas. The native clematis is especially eye-catching in spring.
- A wide range of native birdlife is abundant depending on the time of year, such as korimako (bellbird), riroriro (grey warbler), piwakawaka (fantail), silvereye, brown creeper, kereru (wood-pigeon), shining cuckoo and rifleman.

10 Mt Thomas Forest: Loop 2 Circuit

GRADE 2

TIME One hour return.

ACCESS From Rangiora, cross the Ashley River/Rakahuri, then take the road to Lowburn and Glentui until you reach Hayland Road (just before the Garry River). The junction is well signposted to the carpark, and the tracks start on either side of the ford.

TRACK NOTES

From the top carpark take the main Wooded Gully track as it crosses a bridge, then passes the two Loop 1 junctions to reach the Loop 2 junction. Take this track down to the bridge, and then climb to a vehicle road.

The path follows this a short distance, until joining Track 1 from the summit and follows this down to another road. A short side-track cuts down to the carpark.

POINTS OF INTEREST

- At the Mt Thomas road-end there is a sheltered and pleasant camping area, with extensive grass terraces. Toilets, picnic tables and an information board are found here.
- The beech forest is mostly mountain beech, with scattered podocarps at lower levels. There is a pleasant rest and picnic spot beside the top Loop 2 bridge.
- Plenty of other short family walks are found here, including the Red Pine Track, Cherry Lane Track and the Loop 1 Track.

11 Mt Thomas Forest: Wooded Gully and Peak

GRADE 3

TIME 4–6 hours return to the summit.

ACCESS Directions as for Mt Thomas: Forest Loop 2 Circuit above.

TRACK NOTES

From the top carpark, the Wooded Gully track crosses a bridge and climbs past numerous track junctions before descending back towards the creek again. This track, that can seem deceptively long, climbs steadily in zig-zags to the main ridge.

Once on the ridge, turn right and the track leaves the beech forest, crossing open tussock slopes to the summit. An alternative route is via Track 1, a rapid descent through pine forest that is signposted from the summit.

POINTS OF INTEREST

- Views from the tussock grasslands and alpine herbfields from the summit at Mt Thomas (1023 m) are worthwhile, including sights of the Port Hills/Te Poho-o-Tamatea, Kaikouras and the Puketeraki Range.

12 Mt Thomas Forest: Glentui Waterfall Loop

GRADE 2

TIME Five minutes to the waterfall, or one hour return for the Loop Track.

ACCESS From Rangiora, cross the Ashley River/Rakahuri, then take the road to Lowburn and 20 km (past the main entrance to Mt Thomas Forest at Hayland Road) to Glentui itself, just over the Glentui River. Follow the narrow, unsealed Glentui Bush Road past the Glentui Camp roughly 2.5 km to the spacious carpark and picnic area.

Alternatively, from Christchurch take Tram Road to Oxford, and turn onto the Ashley Gorge Road then some 15 km to the Glentui turn-off. Either route is roughly 60 km from Christchurch.

TRACK NOTES

It is only a short distance along the track to the lovely leap of Glentui Falls, which plunges down a cool, mossy chasm.

Take the other track option as it meets the main Richardson Mountains Track for a short distance, until it branches off again. The track crosses the stream above the waterfall and wanders in beech forest down-river, passing the junction with the Bypass Track before continuing across another foot-bridge back up to the carpark.

POINTS OF INTEREST

- There is a delightful, sheltered picnic area at Glentui, but watch out for wasps in late summer. They feed on the honeydew from the beech forest. Camping is permitted.

13 Richardson Mountains and Blowhard Circuit

GRADE 4

TIME 5–7 hours full circuit, 3–4 hours return to Richardson Mountains.

ACCESS As for Mt Thomas Forest: Glentui Waterfall Loop (12) above.

TRACK NOTES

This is a fine day walk, starting and ending at the Glentui picnic area. The track climbs steadily through beech forest to Richardson Mountains (1047 m), on to the tussock tops with good views over the Lees Valley.

The good views continue along the ridge, though the track is a little unclear at some points. Beech and tussock give way to an extensive area of burnt tree stumps that gives a bizarre but not unattractive effect.

The Bypass Track turn-off to Glentui is well marked so be careful not to miss it, otherwise you will continue on the Blowhard Track to a different road end at the Boy's Brigade Camp. It is a long descent through beech forest again to the Glentui Loop Track, where you can choose to walk up or downstream to get back to the carpark.

POINTS OF INTEREST
- Before the Lees Valley gorge road was constructed, the Blowhard Track was used as a stock route, and cattle and sheep were driven right over the mountain tops.

14 Oxford Forest: Ryde Falls

GRADE 2

TIME 2–3 hours return from View Hill carpark.

ACCESS To reach View Hill carpark from Oxford about 2 km further on SH 72, and just across the Eyre River bridge, turn onto Woodstock Road. Then turn onto Ingrams Road, then Perhams Road across the Eyre River ford, and finally onto Wharfedale Track Road through several gates up to the top carpark. Take a passenger for all those gates!

TRACK NOTES

A sheltered bush walk, which is suitable for families, to an attractive 3-step waterfall. From View Hill carpark follow the main Wharfedale Track (15) past one junction to the signposted second. Follow this track down to Cooper's Creek and pass another junction, then cross the creek up to the pretty Ryde Falls.

On the return, take the track alternative, climbing past an information board and join the main Cooper's Creek Track. Turn uphill back to View Hill carpark. The track junctions are numerous but are all well signposted.

POINTS OF INTEREST
- Oxford Forest was part of Harewood Forest, originally 140,000 ha but presently a much slimmer 11,750 ha. At one time, this old forest nearly reached Oxford township. A newspaper advertisement of 1860 ran: 'For Sale, a 20 acre section, 8 acres of bush situated at Oxford about 3 minutes walk from the township ...'
- The forest is black beech and, higher up, mountain beech, interspersed with podocarps such as rimu, matai and kahikatea (known as 'red pine', 'black pine', and 'white pine' to early European settlers). Sawmilling started here in 1854, with over 11 mills working during the 1870s.

15 Oxford Forest: Wharfedale Track

GRADE 3

TIME 6–8 hours one-way, including the last section of farm track across Mt Pember Station to Lees Valley Road.

ACCESS To reach View Hill carpark from Oxford, drive further along SH 72 and just after the Eyre River bridge turn onto Woodstock Road. Then turn onto Ingrams Road, then Perhams Road, across the Eyre River ford, and finally onto Wharfedale Track Road through several gates up to the top carpark. Access to the Lees Valley end of the Wharfedale Track is via the Oxford township, on to Ashley Gorge Road, and after 5 km turn onto Lees Valley Road. This is a long, winding and highly scenic road, about 20 km to where the other end of the Wharfedale Track is signposted. Walking access only from here, unless permission for a vehicle has been granted by the station owners.

TRACK NOTES

It takes a day to follow the Wharfedale Track from View Hill carpark to Lees Valley Road. If you can arrange transport it is very easy-going travel. This track is popular with mountain bikers.

The track is broad at first, passing several track junctions, and crosses several stream gullies as it winds in and out of bush up to a low saddle. A track junction is here but the main track continues down to the hut by Dobson Stream. This has six bunks and mattresses.

The track carries on to Townshend Hut, which is run-down. A vehicle track now leads out to the Lees Valley Road, and if you do not mind wet feet this is quicker than the flood track option.

POINTS OF INTEREST

- The Wharfedale Track was originally built as a road in 1879 for accessing Lees Valley.
- A surveyor in the 1860s complained of the Wharfedale as 'mud to horses knees, track awful', but today the track is dry, pleasant and shady.

16 Mt Oxford Peak

GRADE 4

TIME 7–8 hours from View Hill carpark or Cooper's Creek.

ACCESS From Christchurch take Tram Road to Oxford township. About 1 km past Oxford turn onto Woodside Road, and follow the signposts some 7 km to Mountain Road and Cooper's Creek carpark.

TRACK NOTES

Mt Oxford is a very strenuous full day round-trip, with a long open tops walk section, but tracks are well marked. From Cooper's Creek carpark the track starts on 'Track 1', then immediately crosses Cooper's Creek and follows a farm track past Beehive Flat and up to the Payton Scout Lodge.

Above the lodge the track zig-zags down to the east branch of Cooper's Creek, then follows along a low beech spur for some way. Past the tramway junction the spur starts to climb through more beech and into open scrub, gradually getting into snow tussocks higher up.

A beacon stands on the high point (1356 m) and a poled route takes you down a spur that changes from tussock to beech, to a junction with the Wharfedale Track. From here follow the main Cooper's Creek Track back to the carpark.

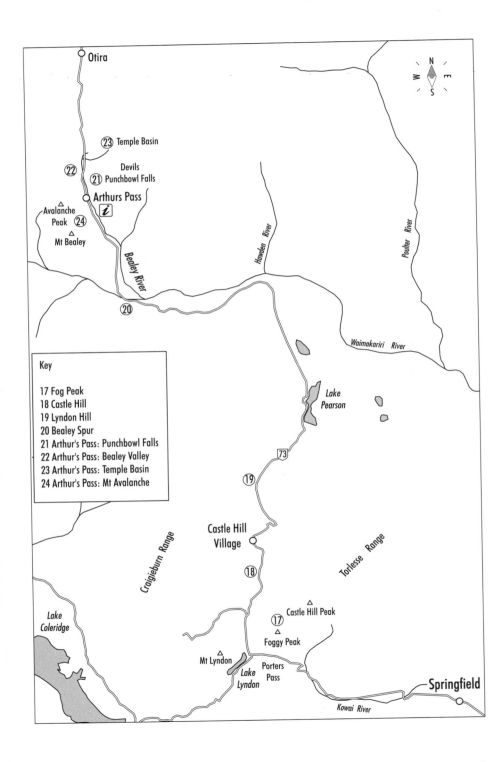

Inland Canterbury and Arthur's Pass

Once you cross the foothills at Porters Pass – which, incidentally, is higher than Arthur's Pass – SH 73 leads you into a fascinating area of expansive high-country landscapes and big mountain scenery.

Here are some of Canterbury's best walks: either fossicking in the limestone country of Castle Hill; or testing yourself on the rugged arid slopes of the Torlesse Range; or exploring the waterfalls and mountains around Arthur's Pass village.

Access to these day walks is generally extremely easy, with usually a carpark found beside the main highway. All walks are signposted. It is sensible to pick good weather for the more exposed mountain walks, such as Fog Peak (17) or Mt Avalanche (24).

17 Fog Peak

GRADE 3 to 4

TIME 3–4 hours return.

ACCESS SH 73 at Porters Pass.

TRACK NOTES

This is an exposed but invigorating alpine walk. Porters Pass is situated at 942 m and the total climb is 800 m to Fog Peak. There is no formal track marked, but from the information board, worn trails wind through the low sub-alpine heathfields to the tussock and rock slopes above. Occasional cairns also mark the way to the peak at 1741 m.

Because of the informal nature of the track, this route should be attempted only in fine weather. *Walkers should carry a topographic map, water and warm clothing.*

POINTS OF INTEREST

- This area is now part of the Korowai/Torlesse Tussocklands Park, which covers approximately 21,000 ha. There are few formal tracks or routes in the park at present.
- This area was important to Maori for food gathering, and a network of trails existed. The name Korowai (cloak) is symbolic of the ancestral connection that tribes, from the early Waitaha to present day Ngai Tahu, have with this region.

ABOVE: An ideal day to take in views by the cairn on Fog Peak (17).

- Charles Torlesse was a surveyor with the Canterbury provincial government, and in 1849 was led by local Maori guides on a climb over the slopes of this range. The first European track over Porters Pass was made by pick and shovel from 1858–59.

18 Castle Hill

GRADE 1
TIME 1–2 hours wandering return.
ACCESS From SH 73 by roadside signpost. There is no proper off-road parking so be watchful of cars on the highway.
TRACK NOTES
From the gate follow the worn trail past matagouri scrub to the base of the cliffs. You can scramble in any direction, and by skirting the lime quarry and the fenced reserve can climb 150 m to Castle Hill itself. A prominent clump of pinnacles stands on top, the tallest up to 12 m high. Carry your own water.

A fascinating place to explore, and the size of the stones is deceptive from the road. It is only when you walk among them that their true scale emerges.

ABOVE: Day walkers heading towards the fascinating limestone formations at Castle Hill (18).

RIGHT: Godley Head Circuit (33) is one of the most popular recreational areas near Christchurch.

BELOW: Pausing by the bushline on Scott's Track, on the way to Avalanche Peak (24).

ABOVE: Signpost beside Sign of the Kiwi (35).

ABOVE: Family trip to Coopers Knob (36), Port Hills.

ABOVE: Grandmother and grandaughter atop Big Rock, Orton Bradley Park (40), looking towards Lyttleton Harbour/Whakaraupo.

ABOVE: Spectacular evening clouds in the Canterbury high country.

RIGHT: Hot day in the Hooker Valley with Aoraki/Mt Cook in the distance (61).

ABOVE: Winter snowfall (2003) on trees at start of Methven Walkway (46).

ABOVE: Day walker arriving at Red Tarn (63), with Aoraki/Mt Cook behind.

POINTS OF INTEREST

- *Kura Tawhiti: treasure from afar*, a DoC pamphlet, details the spiritual and cultural significance of this area for Maori. Charcoal drawings dated to 500 years ago have been discovered and this area was used for seasonal food gathering. Kiore (Polynesian rat), a 'favoured food of Ngai Tahu', was the main food hunted at Kura Tawhiti. They were preserved in their own fat, particularly after prolific beech-seeding years that resulted in a population explosion of kiore.

- Geologically, Castle Hill basin is complex. The Torlesse Range and Craigieburn Range are mostly greywacke, but Castle Hill is a layered mixture of sandstone, siltstone, glacial gravels and even coal measures. The prominent limestone ridges have weathered better than the surrounding rock.

- Castle Hill's geological formations, and Cave Stream, are examples of karst topography. 'Karst' takes its name from the Yugoslavian formation that was first used to describe what results when limestone is dissolved by weak acids in the groundwater. The water makes unusual pathways into the ground and leaves behind the characteristic sinkhole or tomo (the Maori word for these depressions).

19 Craigieburn Forest: Lyndon Hill

GRADE 2

TIME 2–3 hours return.

ACCESS About 110 km from Christchurch along SH 73, turn into Broken River Skifield Road and continue to the shelter and carpark.

TRACK NOTES

An attractive beech forest walk takes you up to the hill lookout, with a different track option to return on. From the carpark cross the footbridge over Cave Stream, as the track wanders past an excellent grass camping area and up through beech forest to the four-way junction on Lyndon Saddle.

By turning right you will encounter a short steep climb to the top of Lyndon Hill (1262 m), once known as Helicopter Hill.

Good views are to be had over the Broken River basin and the Craigieburn cutting, once known as Iona Pass, which separates the Broken River and Waimakariri catchments.

Return down to the saddle, and here you can follow another track around to the road and walk back down Broken River Skifield Road to the carpark.

ABOVE: The impressive view from Lyndon Hill (19) to Craigieburn Range.

20 Bealey Spur

GRADE 3

TIME 3–4 hours return to Bealey Spur Hut.

ACCESS From SH 73, just after Bruce Stream bridge, drive up the steep access road through the Bealey baches to the small carpark and signpost.

TRACK NOTES

Bealey Spur offers a gradual climb from the carpark through silver beech and, later, mountain beech forest to wide-ranging views of the Southern Alps. This path then follows poles out of the manuka belt onto an area burnt-off for grazing. The views are impressive.

Once over a tussock knoll, the track drops through a beech copse and follows a boardwalk across a pretty wetland. In winter these tarns freeze over, but in summer they host a wealth of bog plants such as sundews.

From the wetland, the track climbs through open tussocks to the beech forest festooned with a white, hanging lichen. It is then a short climb through forest to Bealey Spur Hut.

POINTS OF INTEREST

- Like pohutukawa and rata, parita (mistletoe) is a 'Christmas' plant, flowering in a red outburst of colour among the drabber silver beech, which is its common host. Parita is a hemi-parasite (part-parasite), as it photosynthesises its own food but extracts minerals and water from the beech tree. Unfortunately, because the possum seems to be particularly fond of parita, this attractive plant is becoming an increasingly rare sight on Bealey Spur.
- The old shepherd's hut was built in 1925 on a frame of pole beech, and named the Top Hut. It was formerly part of the Cora Lynn Station where the sheep were gathered for the autumn muster.

21 Arthur's Pass: Punchbowl Falls

GRADE 2

TIME One hour return.

ACCESS Arthur's Pass is 150 km from Christchurch on SH 73, and the Punchbowl Falls carpark is at the north end of the village, signposted 200 m down a sideroad. The entrance is just past the Chalet Restaurant. This is also the carpark for the Bridal Veil Falls.

TRACK NOTES

From the carpark, the well-marked track follows the bank of the Bealey River to the long footbridge and the junction with the Bridal Veil Falls Track. The Punchbowl Falls track crosses a second footbridge and there is a reasonable view of the powerful, attractive waterfall from here.

The track then climbs steeply, passing the side-track to Mt Aicken, and turning in to the narrow stream valley to the base of the falls. Signs warn of rockfall, but you can go further to reach the large pool at the base of the 131 m falls, and get drenched by bursts of spray.

POINTS OF INTEREST

- Arthur's Pass was sometimes used by Maori as a pounamu (greenstone) trading route, but the pass was only discovered by Europeans in 1864 by the Dobson brothers George and Arthur (though Samuel Butler reputedly identified the pass as early as 1860). A dray road was cut through to the West Coast by 1865 to supply the newly discovered gold diggings.
- In 1909 a small hydro-power station was built at the foot of the Punchbowl Stream to generate power for the construction of the railway tunnel. Water was taken from the top of the falls via pipes and tunnels down the steep hill. The electricity was used for lighting, air compressors and water pumps in the tunnel. The powerhouse was removed in 1929.
- Another good walk in this area is Bridal Veil Falls, which starts off the Punchbowl Falls track. Allow one hour 30 minutes return. **Note:** It is safer to return on the track rather than along the narrow highway.

22 Arthur's Pass: Bealey Valley

GRADE 3

TIME 1–2 hours return to the top section of Bealey River.

ACCESS The track starts from a carpark, 2 km north of the village, off SH 73.

TRACK NOTES

This is a pretty, quiet and enclosed valley, and the track starts by sidling down and over the bridge across the turbulent Bealey River, aptly referred to as The Chasm. Then the track climbs to an attractive tarn and wetland area which is crossed via boardwalks making this first part of the track ideally suited to families with young children.

ABOVE: Bridge across 'The Chasm' at Bealey River (22).

From here the track gets rougher, and it scrambles up the side of the river, eventually becoming smoother along the rocky riverbed.

If you are feeling adventurous, and do not mind wet feet, you can scramble up the riverbed for an hour to see waterfalls gushing down the top of Bealey River. Old avalanche snow accumulates in this valley, and can linger through to early summer.

POINTS OF INTEREST

- The DoC Visitor Centre is worth a visit, with an original Cobb & Co. coach and many other interesting exhibits on show. If you are considering a trip above the bushline then you should consult the staff at the visitor centre at Arthur's Pass for reliable weather information and track conditions.
- Samuel Bealey was the third superintendent of the Canterbury Provincial Council, and it was his name that Arthur Dudley Dobson and his brother saw fit to bestow on half a dozen landmarks in 1864, as they passed through on their way to the yet to be rediscovered Arthur's Pass.

23 Arthur's Pass: Temple Basin

GRADE 4

TIME 2–3 hours return to the shelter.

ACCESS From Arthur's Pass village, drive 4 km to the Temple Basin carpark and the signposted walk.

TRACK NOTES

Choose a fine day for this exposed walk, and take a camera as the views of the waterfalls, mountains and Mt Rolleston are hard to beat.

From the large carpark follow the steep four-wheel-drive (4WD) road, which narrows to a zig-zag track. This clambers up past bluffs and a good waterfall to the top tussock slopes and the skifield complex. There is a good lunch shelter here with toilets and running water in summer.

POINTS OF INTEREST

- This track is also the main walkway and entrance to the Temple Basin skifield, though skis and other equipment are carted up by a precarious goods lift. Needless to say, you have to be hardy to ski here, particularly in winter when the track is covered with snow and hard ice. Crampons have to be used on occasion just to gain access to the skifield.

- Birds in the mountains are relatively few, but you should see the kea (mountain parrot), the large black-backed gull or New Zealand pipit, identified by its characteristic bobbing and dipping motion. The early settlers and travellers called them 'snow thrushes', and these are extraordinarily versatile, found from the shoreline to the snowline.
- Another attractive, short walk in this area is the Dobson Nature Walk (one hour 30 minutes return). It also starts from the Temple Basin carpark, and wanders across the flat pass area through alpine plants and tarns. This walk is particularly attractive in late spring when the alpine flowers are out.

24 Arthur's Pass: Mt Avalanche

GRADE 4

TIME 6–8 hours return to the summit.

ACCESS There are two track options, but most people will start up the gentler Scotts Track, found 500 m north of the Arthur's Pass village, and come down the steep track that exits by the DoC visitor centre. *It is strongly recommended that you check first with the DoC Visitor Centre about the weather and track conditions.*

TRACK NOTES

This is properly a tramping trip above the bush edge and you will need full equipment, map, food and warm clothing. Reaching the very top of Avalanche Peak (1100 m) is a hard day's walk, but many people find it satisfying to climb up to the bush edge. The views from here are wonderful.

From SH 73, the rather rough Scotts Track initially scrambles up through beech forest, and parts of the track are quite rutted. However it gets less steep as the trail gains the main spur and climbs steadily some 500 m to the bush edge. There are good views over the village.

The track is poled as it climbs through the alpine tussock basins to the narrow summit. An alternative descent follows another well poled spur east of the peak, and the going is straightforward to the bushline. Then the track becomes steep as it twists past waterfalls on the sharp descent to the DoC visitor centre.

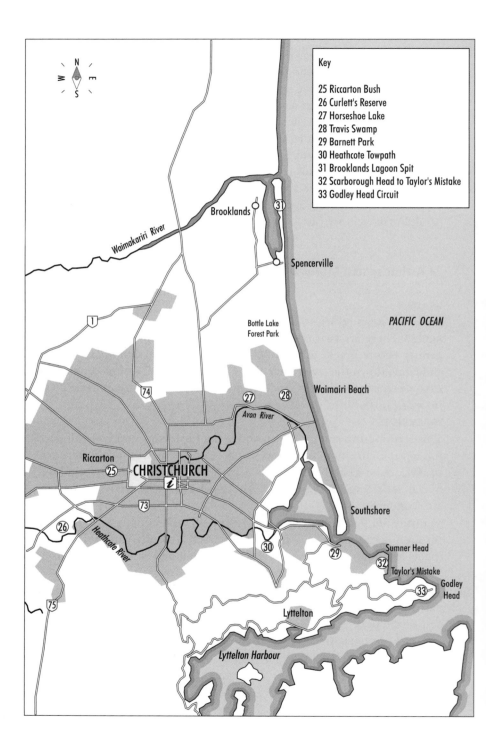

Key

25 Riccarton Bush
26 Curlett's Reserve
27 Horseshoe Lake
28 Travis Swamp
29 Barnett Park
30 Heathcote Towpath
31 Brooklands Lagoon Spit
32 Scarborough Head to Taylor's Mistake
33 Godley Head Circuit

Brooklands

Waimakariri River

Spencerville

PACIFIC OCEAN

Bottle Lake
Forest Park

Waimairi Beach

Avon River

Riccarton

CHRISTCHURCH

Southshore

Heathcote River

Sumner Head

Taylor's Mistake

Godley
Head

Lyttelton

Lyttelton Harbour

Christchurch city

Christchurch city has a population of some 320,000, making it the largest urban area in the South Island. The city is known for its many parks and carefully maintained household gardens, but Christchurch also has many good day walks that explore the quiet, scenic corners of the city.

These walks are ideal for family expeditions and give a sample of the surprisingly varied terrain found either inside or just outside the city boundaries. They include walks alongside rivers, seacliff headlands, saltwater lagoons, rural scenery and native forest.

25 Riccarton Bush

GRADE 1

TIME 15–30 minutes return.

ACCESS In the suburb of Riccarton, off Kahu Road and down a side-road to Riccarton House.

TRACK NOTES

An easy stroll around this secluded bush on well made paths. There are short walks among the 400 or so kahikatea trees and a discrete seating area in a forest enclave underneath the tall trees.

POINTS OF INTEREST

- The Maori name for the forest is Putaringamotu meaning 'the place of an echo' or 'the severed ear'. The latter is a figurative expression referring to the bush's isolation from any other forest.
- Putaringamotu (or Riccarton Bush or Deans Bush as it is also known) is a tiny 7.7 ha fragment of the original podocarp forest of the Canterbury Plains. At the time of the initial European settlement of Christchurch there were only two small copses of forest on the empty plain of Christchurch: Deans Bush and Papanui Bush. The latter has long been demolished, but the Deans family preserved this precious remnant and gifted it to the public in 1914. An Act of Parliament of 1917 protects Putaringamotu.
- Kahikatea is New Zealand's tallest native tree and releases the heaviest seed crop of any podocarp – up to 130 kg. There is a proposal to predator-fence this bush to provide a haven for native birds such as

kereru (wood pigeon), piwakawaka (fantail), korimako (bellbird) and silver eyes.

- Deans Cottage was built by the Deans brothers, John and William, in 1843–44 and is the oldest remaining building in Canterbury.
- The stately Riccarton mansion was built in stages from the 1860s to 1900, and is currently a function centre and restaurant.

26 Curletts Reserve

GRADE 1

TIME 30 minute circuit.

ACCESS Either from Templetons Road, or the halfway entrance from Warren Crescent.

TRACK NOTES

This is an easy trail along the replanted Heathcote River and around the pond, which has two islands that are home to a range of birdlife.

BELOW: Wigram Retention Basin lake at Curletts Reserve (26) is a new home to many bird species.

From Templetons Road carpark, the track crosses a footbridge and closely follows the pleasant bush riverside. It crosses two more footbridges before the junction with the Warren Crescent side track, and from here you can climb to the broad stopbank of the lake.

A circular track goes around the lake and returns you directly back to Templetons Road; or, follow the marker poles along the track down the Heathcote River to Curletts Road and take Halswell Road back to Templetons Road.

POINTS OF INTEREST

- The formal name for this man-made lake is the Wigram Retention Basin and, as its name suggests, it is a flood protection work to prevent flooding in the upper Heathcote River. Native plantings of toe toe and sedges have disguised the pond's origins, and has created a popular wetland for several species of ducks, scaup, gulls and black swans.

27 Horseshoe Lake

GRADE 1

TIME One hour full-circuit.

ACCESS There are several carparks off Lake Terrace Road in the suburb of Burwood, about 5 km from Cathedral Square.

TRACK NOTES

An ideal day walk for families, this is an easy saunter around the inner curve of Horseshoe Lake, and a return across a section of woodland.

From the carpark, walk around the west end of the lake past the junction with the Woodland Walk, and follow the inner curve of the lake. Sections of boardwalk lead you to a seat by Rearby Street junction, and slightly further is a picnic area and shelter.

Take the Rearby Track along to Rearby Street, turn left along Queensbury Street then right into Goodman Street to Broomfield Terrace, and a short way further to the start of the Woodland Walk. This leads across a wetland (which sometimes floods in heavy rain) and boardwalks back to the start of the Horseshoe Lake carpark.

POINTS OF INTEREST

- Horseshoe Lake was once a loop of the Avon River/Otakaro and is a classic ox-bow lake, created when the main current of the river found a more direct line of fall. In pre-European times it was the site of a Maori settlement, Te Oranga, and the lake was named Waikakariki.

ABOVE: Waterfowl on Horseshoe Lake (27).

- The reserve was created in 1904 and birdlife found here includes mallard duck, Canada Goose, grey duck, New Zealand shoveller, little shag, welcome swallow, New Zealand scaup and kingfisher.

28 Travis Wetland

GRADE 1

TIME One to two hours return.

ACCESS There are several entrances to the circular track around Travis Wetland. The information kiosk, carpark and bird-hide are off Beach Road. Angela's Stream is off Travis Road with carparking on the broad grass verge. Access to the Anne Flanagan section of the walkway is via the carpark off Mairehau Road. The closest access to the bird observation tower is off Travis Country Drive. **Note:** At present the circular track has not been completed, but may be finished in 2005.

TRACK NOTES

From Beach Road carpark you can visit the bird-hide (ten minutes) but the main track continues north around to a side track to Inwoods Road. The next section of walkway continues round to Mairehau Road

ABOVE: Boardwalk over the wetland of Travis Swamp (28).

carpark, then continues on boardwalks through willow forest to the bird observation tower.

The last section of track continues to Clarevale Reserve and follows the pretty Angela's Stream around to Travis Road. There you will find a gap in the track network, and can walk briefly along the busy Travis Road to Frosts Road then back to the Beach Road carpark. Otherwise, return back along the circular track.

POINTS OF INTEREST

- Anne Flanagan was an early environmental campaigner who inspired the Travis Wetland Trust.
- Travis Wetland (or Travis Swamp as it was commonly known) was bought by the Christchurch City Council in 1997 after a battle to save the area from housing development. The wisdom of this purchase has been justified with over 60 species recorded in Travis Wetland, including the rare white heron, black stilt, glossy ibis and Australasian bittern.
- When Maori arrived at Travis Wetland c.1300 AD they found a rich feeding ground of water-fowl, native pigeon, eel and fish in an extensive fresh-water wetland of open pools and slow-moving streams. The settlement of Orupaeroa used the abundant raupo for thatching and rafts, and flax for weaving.

ABOVE: The staircase and cave on Barnett Park (29) walkway.

29 Barnett Park

GRADE 2

TIME One hour to one hour 30 minute circuit.

ACCESS The carpark and toilets are found beside the Main Road to Sumner.

TRACK NOTES

This is an easy half-day walk up a short side-valley in the suburb of Redcliffs. Children will enjoy the caves.

From the carpark, the track skirts the sports field to a stile, then cuts a diagonal path across to a power pylon. The track steadily climbs the side of the dry, open valley, passing two seats until reaching a 70-step staircase to an impressive rock cave.

The circuit continues down the other side of the valley and passes several seats and some fragments of bush. Roughly halfway down a side-track leads to the well disguised Paradise Cave. The track completes the loop back at the sports field.

POINTS OF INTEREST

- Maori used the caves and rock shelters in this area to access the food resources of the estuary, though none were inhabited by the time Europeans settled.

- During the 1880s, landowner J.S. Monck allowed the Volunteers (similar to present-day Army Territorials) to use the area for training and military exercises. Regular shooting championships were held here, and the army's use of the area continued through both world wars for training and accommodation. The army transferred the land to the Christchurch City Council in 1954.

30 Heathcote Towpath

GRADE 1

TIME One hour return.

ACCESS The best carparking is found in Settlers Crescent, off Ferry Road.

TRACK NOTES

A pleasant flat walk alongside the lower Heathcote River with viewing platforms and a bird-hide. Good views towards the Port Hills.

From the Settlers Crescent carpark, the track crosses to the information platform, which in 1851 was the site of the historic ferry crossing. The track then winds past the saltmarsh and then passes the sidetrack to Settlers Crescent (a good return route), and meanders across small footbridges over the tidal inlets eventually meeting Ferry Road near the bollard monument.

POINTS OF INTEREST

- This is an historic section of waterway, as in the 1850s and 1860s the Heathcote River was deep enough to allow small boats to reach wharves several kilometres from the river mouth. At that time Woolston was the main port of entry to Christchurch, with at least five separate wharves. The bird-hide also marks the spot of Devils Elbow, an awkward kink in the river where boats were frequently towed by horses utilising the towpath.

31 Brooklands Lagoon Spit

GRADE 2

TIME 3–4 hours return.

ACCESS Spencer Park, signposted 15 km from Christchurch, can be reached by travelling from Marshland Road onto Lower Styx Road.

ABOVE: At the edge of Brooklands tidal lagoon (31).

TRACK NOTES

Signposted as the Waimakariri Walkway, this day walk follows dune country on the inside of the spit that separates Brooklands Lagoon from the sea. Start opposite the main picnic area beside the bird observation tower and follow the inner curve of the lagoon as it winds through sandy dune and scrub country.

There are several sidetracks that cross to the shore, so you can exit early on if you wish, however, the main track continues to the Waimakariri River mouth. You can then walk back along the beach for a varied circuit.

POINTS OF INTEREST

- The Brooklands Lagoon is a coastal estuary that has been formed from the merging of the Waimakariri and Styx rivers. It has salt-marsh and sedge communities around the edge and is an important stopover and breeding ground for a large number of bird species.
- Other walks in the Brooklands Lagoon and Spencer Park area include the Wetland Walk (20 minutes), Brooklands Bird Hide (40 minutes) and the Southern Pegasus Bay Track (two hours one-way). All walks are signposted and marked on information boards beside the entrance road. There are also mountain bike trails in Bottle Lake Forest.

ABOVE: Day walkers overlooking steep sea-cliffs on the track to Scarborough Head (32).

32 Scarborough Head to Taylor's Mistake

GRADE 2

TIME Two hours return.

ACCESS Take the Scarborough Road towards Taylor's Mistake, and turn off at the carpark beside Nicholson Park. Picnic area and toilets are found here.

TRACK NOTES

This is a raw and dramatic walk along the cliff edge of Scarborough to the sandy bay of Taylor's Mistake. Some parts of the track are narrow, and can get slippery and muddy after rain.

From Nicholson Park, cross the road and take the broad berm down to the sudden cliffside. The track forks here, and the left track goes to Sumner via steps and Whitewash Head Road, but take the right track to Taylor's Mistake.

The track drops quite quickly down steps and sidles in and out of various gullies and short spurs, and in places the track drops quite close to the sea. The track then climbs around a snub peninsula known as the Giant's Nose,

ABOVE: Paragliding is another way to see Godley Head.

and swings around to Hobson Bay where baches hang improbably off the cliffsides. There is at high tide a high-level track through the baches, but at low tide you can drop down to the beach.

POINTS OF INTEREST

- Spotted shag colonies beside the cliff walk are a wonderful sight, and they are always busy with activity. The main breeding takes place in spring with an average clutch of three eggs. Young are ready to leave at nine weeks.

- The word 'bach' is a contraction of 'bachelor'; the word refers to home-built huts that provide a refuge from the busy world, and there are some beauties at Taylor's Mistake. Some of the baches are built on public land and there has been a long-running dispute as to their fate, but they add so much character to the beach it would be shame to see them demolished.

33 Godley Head Circuit

GRADE 3

TIME 4–5 hours full circuit, including tunnel.

ACCESS From Christchurch city it is a 15 km drive on Scarborough Road to Taylor's Mistake beach. Picnic area and toilets are found here.

TRACK NOTES

There are excellent views and an equally interesting history on this headland, which is one of the most popular recreational areas in Christchurch. Good area for families. Remember that several of these tracks are designated multi-use, which means they are shared with mountain bikers.

At the far end of Taylor's Mistake beach, the broad track climbs around and along the headlands to the tiny baches at Boulder Bay. There will be a steady climb from here to the ridge and Summit Road.

You could continue along the ridge tracks, but it is worthwhile descending the track to the tunnel beside Lyttelton Harbour/Whakaraupo. The track goes past the remains of old military buildings (also a sidetrack to a coastal lookout), then descends sharply to a 110-m-long tunnel that can be walked through to the searchlight emplacements.

Back on the main ridge, follow the track as it sidles evenly along the tussock peninsula, past a lookout, then down to Breeze Col. From here, the track is shared with mountain bikers and again drops back down to Taylor's Mistake.

POINTS OF INTEREST

- Maori knew of Godley Head as Otokitoki, meaning 'the place of trees and birds', but the Europeans named it after John Robert Godley, co-founder of the Canterbury Association and undisputed leader of the Canterbury Settlement. An early name was Cachalot Head, perhaps named after a French whaling ship *Cachalot*. Cachalot is French for sperm whale. The French corvette *Heroine* visited Port Cooper (Lyttelton) in 1838.

- White-flippered blue penguin are found along this coast in several nesting sites, particularly at Boulder Bay. More nesting boxes have been provided at other sites along the coast in order to make the population sustainable.

- In 1939 two six-inch gun batteries were built on Godley Head, with a third battery following in 1942 (at the height of the Japanese invasion scare). The first two had overhead concrete covers but the third was open with a 360° firing arc. The lighthouse was shifted to clear the field of fire, and the battery had radar able to scan halfway to Wellington. Searchlight emplacements were built at sea level to shine across the harbour entrance and the tunnel dug to give foot access to them. Concrete magazines, barracks, mess halls and a kitchen were also built for the 11th Coast Regiment.

- Several of the caves along the coast to Boulder Bay were occupied in the 1890s, mostly as weekend retreats by some interesting characters: 'The three Kennedy brothers, well-known mountaineers, are thought to have been the first to camp in caves here, and by the 1890s Thomas Archbold had made one into a comfortable house, complete with rainwater-supply and fireplace. Next door in 1903 came Alfred Osborne, known as 'The Pilgrim', who had a telephone line to his neighbour held by insulators made from lemonade bottles ... Probably the most impressive was one called the Hermitage, whose main cave was 60ft by 25ft and 14ft high. It was fitted out by two men, Cameron and Cropp, with material salvaged from the 1906 Exhibition, and was later bought by a city dentist, Jesse Worgan, who furnished it with a piano, brought around from Sumner by rowing-boat'. Source: *Sumner to Ferrymead* (1976) by Walter de Thier.

ABOVE: Looking down at Boulder Bay on Godley Head walkway (33).

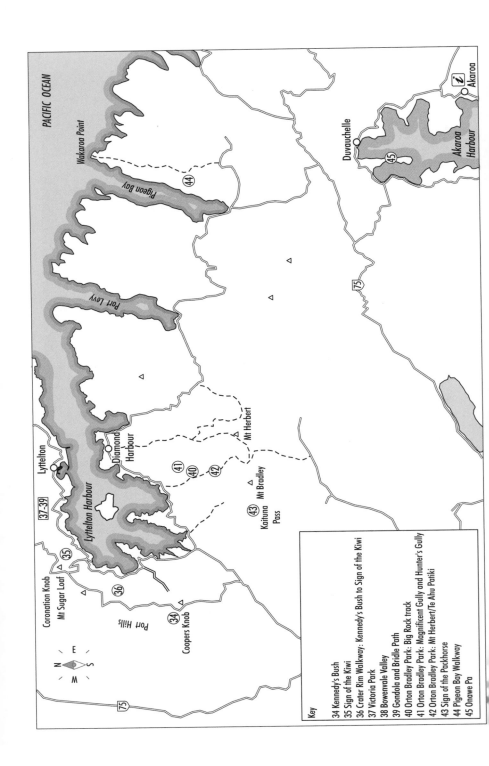

PACIFIC OCEAN

Wakaroa Point

Pigeon Bay

Port Levy

Lyttelton

37-39

Lyttelton Harbour

Diamond Harbour

⑪41
⑫42
⑩40

Mt Herbert

Mt Bradley
⑬43
Kaituna Pass

Duvauchelle

⑮45

Akaroa Harbour

ⓘ
Akaroa

Coronation Knob
Mt Sugar Loaf
⑤35

⑥36

Port Hills

Coopers Knob
④34

75

75

N
W — E
S

Key

34 Kennedy's Bush
35 Sign of the Kiwi
36 Crater Rim Walkway: Kennedy's Bush to Sign of the Kiwi
37 Victoria Park
38 Bowenvale Valley
39 Gondola and Bridle Path
40 Orton Bradley Park: Big Rock track
41 Orton Bradley Park: Magnificent Gully and Hunter's Gully
42 Orton Bradley Park: Mt Herbert/Te Ahu Patiki
43 Sign of the Packhorse
44 Pigeon Bay Walkway
45 Onawe Pa

Port Hills and Banks Peninsula

The Port Hills provide Christchurch's distinctive signature skyline and offer huge opportunities for walking. A track network encompasses nearly all of these hills, and there are walks available from easy family strolls to harder daytramps.

There are some extensive and healthy stands of native bush to explore on the Lyttelton harbourside, with good populations of native birds. The views everywhere are magnificent, particularly on a fine winter's day where the Southern Alps stand crisply over the Canterbury Plains.

Both the Port Hills and Banks Peninsula share the same volcanic geology, with distinctive rock outcrops and sharp bluffs. Banks Peninsula was created by two large volcanoes that subsequently became occupied by the sea as Lyttelton and Akaroa harbours. Curiously, Captain James Cook called Banks Peninsula 'Bank's Island', but he was a mere 20,000 years too late to call it such; that was when the eroded gravels from the Southern Alps finally reached the peninsula and joined it to the mainland.

Banks Peninsula has several good walking areas, notably based around Orton Bradley Park and the summit crest. You could spend many weekends exploring all the tracks on the Port Hills and Banks Peninsula.

34 Kennedy's Bush

GRADE 2

TIME One hour circuit.

ACCESS Drive along Summit Road to the Sign of the Bellbird, a stone resthouse, where there are toilets and a picnic area.

TRACK NOTES

This is a fine stand of bush on the Port Hills that includes several specimens of totara trees and a maze of tracks. The outer track is reasonably well signposted, and if you do get lost just keep taking the uphill tracks.

From the Sign of the Bellbird, take the track past the toilet as it loops downhill, passing three other track junctions on the right. Keep to the main trail as it descends a long way into the bush valley to a fork at the stream.

Now the track starts climbing again, past a big totara tree, and crosses the stream twice as it ascends slowly back to Summit Road.

ABOVE: The historic stone rest house, 'The Sign of the Bellbird', in Kennedy's Bush (34).

POINTS OF INTEREST

- The forest is composed mainly of mahoe (whiteywood), kanuka, ribbonwood and kowhai with some totara. Native birds such as kereru (wood pigeon), korimako (bellbird) and shining cuckoo (when in season) can usually be heard.
- The original Sign of the Bellbird was built in 1913 as a caretaker's cottage for the bush reserve, and then extended to make a tearoom in 1915. The tearooms fell into disuse and vandalism during the Second World War. The current shelter was rebuilt from the original stones.

35 Sign of the Kiwi

GRADE 2

TIME One hour to one hour 30 minute circuit (including Mt Sugar Loaf).

ACCESS Drive up Dyers Pass Road roughly 8 km to the carpark beside the Sign of the Kiwi.

TRACK NOTES

The start of this walk is over the crossroads, opposite the Sign of the Kiwi, with a stile and sign labelled Mitchells Track. The track divides, so take the right hand track into the bush as it sidles slowly through a substantial hillside of native bush of dominant mahoe, lancewood, broadleaf and tarata (lemonwood), and some tuneful korimako (bellbird) and ririroro (grey warbler). There is a lookout and seat along the way.

It takes roughly 30 minutes to amble up through the bush reserve and past the Smyth seat to the junction with Cedric's Track. Follow this track as it climbs gently across tussocks around to the large Mt Sugar Loaf carpark.

It takes another 20 minutes or so to walk up the sealed road to the summit of Mt Sugar Loaf (496 m) and television tower. From here you can look along the entire length of the volcanic escarpment of the Port Hills.

Back down at Mt Sugar Loaf carpark, pick up the other half of Cedric's Track that travels easily down to the Sign of the Kiwi again.

POINTS OF INTEREST

- Other walks from the Sign of the Kiwi include the track around Coronation Knob (30 minutes return).
- The Maori name for Mt Sugar Loaf is Te Pohue, a name given to several climbing or trailing plants.
- The name 'sugar loaf' features on many New Zealand hills, and is an old-fashioned name for a large conical mass of hard refined sugar, so

ABOVE: Sidling on Ella's Track under Mt Ada, on the Crater Rim Walkway (36).

it has nothing to do with bread. The term dates back at least to the 15th century ('a greate hyghe picke lyke a suger lofe') when sugar was sold in these conical blocks. In the Tudor period there was a fad for high pointed hats, immediately dubbed 'sugar-loaf hats'.

36 Crater Rim Walkway: Kennedy's Bush to Sign of the Kiwi

GRADE 3

TIME One hour 30 minutes to two hours one way.

ACCESS As for Kennedy's Bush (34).

TRACK NOTES

The Crater Rim Walkway runs along the top ridge of the Port Hills from Cooper's Knob to Godley Head, and provides first-class views. This is one section of the track from the Sign of the Bellbird (Kennedy's Bush) to the Sign of the Kiwi. The track is often marked with red walkway signposts.

At the Sign of the Bellbird carpark, follow the easy trail around the Lyttelton Harbour side of Mt Ada. This section is known as Ella's Track. The track then follows the Summit Road around to Hoon Hay Park. The main track stays closer to the road, but there is a sidetrack onto Trig V and this continues on to meet the main track again.

The track crosses the summit road (and Worsley's Road) and runs gently downhill, crossing the summit road again. Here, the main track swings away from the road around Coronation Knob, but there is a short-cut alternative. In any case both tracks reach the Sign of the Kiwi, which has toilets and tearooms.

POINTS OF INTEREST

- The Sign of the Kiwi is another old stone rest house that first opened in 1917. It is now an information centre and ranger station, with toilets and (still) a charming, traditional tearoom.

37 Victoria Park: H.G. Ell Track

GRADE 2

TIME Two hours return.

ACCESS On Dyers Pass road, just after the Sign of the Takahe, there is a carpark and the start of the track. However, if this carpark is full there are at least two more carparks within 500 m along the road that all link to the H.G. Ell track.

TRACK NOTES

This is a very popular track, which climbs easily to the Sign of the Kiwi, and has a good alternative route back. The network of tracks is confusing but they all tend to end up at the same places. From the bottom carpark, the H.G. Ell track closely follows the road, but usually stays about 4–5 m above it. Several sidetracks branch off until the track crosses the Victoria Park Road, then winds up past the Skellerup seat and reaches the Summit Road just before the Sign of the Kiwi at Dyers Pass.

Either return by this track, or turn up the Summit Road a short distance and pick up the Thomson multi-use track, which climbs to the main spur. A multiplicity of mountain bike trails are here, but the main track downhill is reasonably clearly marked and winds through exotic forest to the 19th Battalion Memorial Park and on to the main Victoria Park carpark.

You may also pick up the attractive Tawhairaunui trail, or the track through Elizabeth Park. Both tracks will end up at the Sign of the Takahe.

POINTS OF INTEREST

• This track was named after Harry Ell, the local member of parliament who conceived the idea of a series of hostels along the Summit Road from Christchurch to Akaroa. Several were built, including the baronial Sign of the Takahe (now a restaurant), the Sign of the Kiwi (opened in 1917), the Sign of the Bellbird and the remote Sign of the Packhorse in the 1920s. Ell suffered financial difficulties from time to time, and he lived with his wife Ada in both the Sign of the Takahe and the Sign of the Kiwi houses at different stages of his life.

• Other walks in Victoria Park include the elegant Tawhairaunui Wheelchair Walk (20 minutes one-way), the Latters Spur track (30 minutes one way), and the East Side Bush walk (30 minutes one way).

38 Bowenvale Valley

GRADE 3

TIME 3–4 hours return.

ACCESS Bowenvale Avenue carpark is reached off Centaurus Road.

TRACK NOTES

Bowenvale is a long, picturesque valley, and the main track climbs right to the Summit Road. There are numerous track junctions, as some of this track is shared with mountain bikers.

ABOVE: Pleasant woodland on the H.G. Ell Track through Mt Victoria reserve (37).

ABOVE: The easy way up! Gondola pod with Bridle Path saddle (39) in the background.

From the carpark, follow the vehicle track roughly 500 m to a gate and stile, and continue another 500 m upvalley to a second stile and mountain-bike grid. Ignore the various track junctions as the track winds through a shady gorge and across Bowenvale Stream to the footbridge.

The track leaves the pine trees behind and crosses several footbridges as it climbs into an open tussock valley with bluffs and streamside flax. More track junctions to ignore (some for mountain bikers) as the track climbs and finally meets a vehicle track that hauls up to the Summit Road.

39 Gondola and Bridle Path

GRADE 3

TIME 2–3 hours return to the gondola.

ACCESS From Christchurch central city, it is roughly 8 km to the gondola building, and just beside it is the Bridle Path carpark. Picnic tables and a water fountain are found here.

TRACK NOTES

The Bridle Path is a steep, popular walk, and a good workout. It is worth continuing on to the gondola where you can reward yourself with a

ABOVE: Looking towards Bridle Path (39), the gondola on skyline.

cappuccino, or something a little stronger. Obviously if you wish for an easier walk, you can take the gondola up and walk back.

From the carpark, the track (which is also a vehicle road) climbs steadily past seats to the Seymour stone seat and the Kahukura (or Castle Rock) side track. The Bridle Path continues past the information sign to the saddle, where there are seats and the historic shelter dedicated to pioneer women.

Continue along the main Crater Rim Walkway as it climbs steadily to the gondola building, and pick up a side trail that goes around and underneath the gondola pods to the main entrance.

POINTS OF INTEREST
- The Bridle Path was surveyed and constructed in a feverish hurry over the Christmas period of 1850–51, and finished in the second week of January 1851. Captain Joseph Thomas was the principal surveyor for the Canterbury Association, and one of his tasks was cutting a dray road over Evans Pass (193 m) through to the plains from the port in time for the arrival of the first European settlers. After a year, the Sumner Road was still uncompleted and with the settlers due to arrive in December there was an urgent need for some sort of pathway to the plains. It was a tight finish. The Bridle Path was surveyed in November 1850 and the *Charlotte Jane*, the first of the four immigrant ships, arrived

ABOVE: Climbing towards Mt Herbert/Te Ahu Patiki (42).

on 16 December. By January 1851, there was a daily packhorse over the bridle-path, but most people shifted their heavier luggage by boat over the estuary bar and up the Shakespeare (Avon) or Heathcote rivers. Evans Pass Road was finished in 1857.

- Because of the difficulties of accessing Lyttelton either via the Bridle Path or Evans Pass, the Lyttelton Railway Tunnel was started in July 1861 and broke through in May 1867. The first passenger train went through in December 1867. It was a tremendous and costly achievement for the young colony, and cost close to £300,000.
- The gondola was built in 1993 after a lengthy public debate, for it occupies the Mt Cavendish scenic reserve, and special conditions were imposed on the gondola operation. For example, there is no road access directly to the gondola. The gondola building currently houses a cafe and licensed restaurant.

40 Orton Bradley Park: Big Rock Track

GRADE 2

TIME 40 minutes return.

ACCESS Orton Bradley Park is situated on the far side of Lyttelton Harbour/ Whakaraupo, access via Governors Bay and Teddington about 5 km before the settlement of Diamond Harbour. A small entry fee is charged.

ABOVE: Grandmother and grandaughter atop Big Rock, Orton Bradley Park (40), looking towards Lyttleton Harbour/Whakaraupo.

TRACK NOTES

This is only one of many short walks in Orton Bradley Park, and leads to the top of an impressive rock outcrop. Excellent for small children.

From the top carpark, take the main Mt Herbert/Te Ahu Patiki track as it follows paths over several stiles, crosses a footbridge and winds up the valley to a signposted junction. A short way up the Magnificent Gully, a sidetrack goes to the back of the rock outcrop, and with care you can scramble to the top.

POINTS OF INTEREST

- Orton Bradley Farm Park is a 635 ha working farm park, with many notable historic features: an original stone shepherds hut (built 1848), believed to be the oldest stone hut in Canterbury; the Charteris Bay School (founded 1878); a flax mill (built c.1870–90); a quarry (operating 1938–85); a replica of the original homestead, and groves of exotic trees of 159 different species.
- The Reverend Bradley bought the property in 1858 for £1000 and was succeeded by his son Orton in 1892, who lived there for 50 years. Orton was a keen horticulturalist and constructed an ingenious system of water supply; the water was used both for three-tier irrigation for his extensive tree plantings as well as to drive the waterwheel (constructed around 1890–1901 and still in full working condition), which in turn powered a smithy, saw, lathe, drill press, oat crusher and electric lighting. Orton Bradley died in 1943, and left the estate to the people of New Zealand.

41 Orton Bradley Park: Magnificent Gully and Hunters Gully

GRADE 3

TIME Two hours return.

ACCESS As for Orton Bradley Park (40).

TRACK NOTES

This is a longer rural track, offering good views over the park and Lyttelton Harbour/Whakaraupo. The optional Lookout Track should be considered for an interesting way to considerably extend the walk.

Follow the main valley track up to the Big Rock junction, then turn along the shady Magnificent Gully Track. This winds up pleasantly through bush to a junction with the Lookout Track.

Hunters Gully Track winds upwards onto pasture land, with great views, then sidles through conifer forest around to Hunters Gully. This bush gully is full of kanuka and broadleafs, and the kowhai flowers impressively in spring.

The track emerges from the bush, and sidles across a paddock to a stile and adventure playground, then crosses a footbridge to the main carpark.

POINTS OF INTEREST
- The Lookout Track is a steep and strenuous climb, first to an old vehicle track then through a bush gully. Some tree scrambling is needed here, but the track is reasonably defined as it zig-zags through small rock faces and past some big boulders to the open spur. There is a short sidle to a great viewpoint over Orton Bradley Park and Lyttelton Harbour/Whakaraupo. You have climbed so high that you are only a short distance from the main ridge. Return the same way. Allow 1 hour 30 minutes return from the top junction.

42 Orton Bradley Park: Mt Herbert/Te Ahu Patiki

GRADE 4
TIME 6–7 hours return (a full day).
ACCESS As for Orton Bradley Park (40).
TRACK NOTES
This is the premier track in Orton Bradley Park, and climbs to the highest peak (920 m) on Banks Peninsula, which Maori know as Te Ahu Patiki. The track is well marked with poles and occasional signs, though cattle can muddy the trail.

Follow the main valley track as it climbs easily at first along the valley paths and passes various track junctions. Beyond the Waterfall Track turn-off, the track gets steeper and zig-zags through rock bluffs and ribbonwood groves up to the top basin.

Although Mt Herbert/Te Ahu Patiki looks close it is still quite a distance along the 4WD track, as it loops up through gorse fields onto the actual saddle. There is a junction here with the track to Mt Bradley, which is circled by dramatic bluffs.

However, a short climb along the ridge brings you to an open shelter. Then it is a final haul up to the summit. There are superb views of Banks Peninsula, Aoraki/Mt Cook, Lake Ellesmere and the Kaitorete Spit.

Despite the presence of a water tank beside the shelter, do not rely on it and take plenty of water.

ABOVE: The shelter near the summit of Mt Herbert/Te Ahu Patiki (42).

43 Sign of the Packhorse

GRADE 3

TIME 3–4 hours return.

ACCESS Turn off the Christchurch–Akaroa on SH 75 into the Kaituna Valley, down Kaituna Valley Road to a short, unsignposted sideroad roughly 7 km along. A DoC signpost found at the carpark here.

TRACK NOTES

This is an interesting track and not particularly steep, which climbs to the romantically situated Sign of the Packhorse stone hut.

The track initially sidles past the farm buildings, then joins vehicle tracks climbing through a bush-filled valley onto a wide open spur. There are extensive patches of scrub forest in the Kaituna Valley and you can hear quite a few native birds, including kingfishers and korimako (bellbirds). Kanuka trees dominate here, with plenty of kowhai seen also.

After a while, the track sidles onto a farm track past Parkinsons Bush Reserve to the saddle and the Packhorse Hut. The hut was restored (again) by DoC in 2002, equipped with 8 bunks and mattresses, a woodstove and a rainwater tank. In summer the water supply cannot be relied upon, so take your own.

POINTS OF INTEREST

- Banks Peninsula was the unlikely cradle of youth hostelling in New Zealand. The energetic Cora Wilding returned from a trip to Europe, fired up by the concept of hostelling, and helped found the Youth Hostel Association in Christchurch. Walking holidays were popular in the 1920s and 30s, and by 1932 there were as many as 11 hostels on the peninsula with a well-established walking circuit between them.
- The Sign of the Packhorse was built in the 1920s and early photos show a homely place, with curtains by the windows and flowers on the table. It cost a shilling for a bed at the hostel, a shilling for a meal, and lunch (thick bread and butter with cheese) was sixpence.
- A poled track leads behind Mt Bradley and continues to Mt Herbert/ Whakaraupo (920 m), the high point of the peninsula. Another marked route continues down from the Packhorse Hut, pass the Remarkable Dykes (an outcrop of volcanic rock) and then to Gebbies Pass (2–3 hours one way).

44 Pigeon Bay Walkway

GRADE 3

TIME 4–5 hours return.

ACCESS Roughly 80 km from Christchurch (the easiest way is to follow the

BELOW: Wakaroa Point at the end of Pigeon Bay Walkway (44).

ABOVE: Morning light on Onawe Peninsula at Akaroa Harbour.

Christchurch–Akaroa SH 75 to Hilltop) and diverge along the Summit Road to the Pigeon Bay turn-off(45). **Note:** The walkway is closed from August to September for lambing.

TRACK NOTES

This is a dramatic sea cliff overlooking the entrance to Pigeon Bay. The walkway starts from the carpark near the boat jetty and briefly follows the seashore, then climbs through paddocks and a grove of gum trees up to a 4WD vehicle track, which it follows most of the way to Wakaroa Point. The track is well marked with multi-coloured poles, and has pleasant views alongside Pigeon Bay.

From the point you can take in the full sweep of headlands along the peninsula over to Christchurch and the Kaikoura Mountains.

POINTS OF INTEREST

- The Hay Scenic Reserve is also at Pigeon Bay, and is one of the last stands of lowland podocarp forest left on the peninsula – particularly pleasant on a hot day. Fine specimens of matai, kahikatea, totara and miro are mixed with exotics such as pines and poplars, which provide some wind protection to what is a very small reserve (20 minutes return).

ABOVE: Signpost at Onawe Pa (45).

45 Onawe Pa

GRADE 2

TIME One hour return.

ACCESS Drive to Duvauchelle on Christchurch–Akaroa SH 75, then turn onto an unsealed coastal road and travel a kilometre to the small carpark.

TRACK NOTES

Onawe Peninsula offers wonderful coastal scenery, but a mid- to low-tide crossing is essential, otherwise you will get wet feet getting to the 'island'.

At the carpark, a short vehicle track drops to the pebbly beach where you can see striking natural rock patterns on the tidal rocks. Onawe is connected to the mainland by only a razor-thin ridge, which broadens out into a wide grass slope that rises to the beaconed summit, 100 m above sea level.

A good trail climbs to this summit, and the outlook there is excellent. Manuka forest and thick grass now largely obscures the details of the pa site.

POINTS OF INTEREST

- In 1831, Ngai Tahu retreated to this site when they heard of the approach of Te Rauparaha's warriors from the North Island and the subsequent fall of Kaiapoi Pa. Despite the very secure boundaries of the pa and extensive palisades, Te Rauparaha used captured Ngai Tahu men as a shield and broke through the defences. It was said the slaughter was immense, followed by a cannibal feast on the beach.

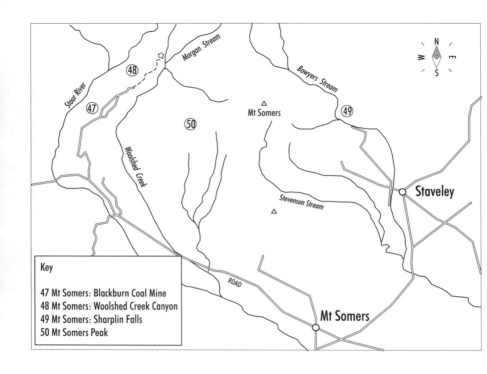

Key

47 Mt Somers: Blackburn Coal Mine
48 Mt Somers: Woolshed Creek Canyon
49 Mt Somers: Sharplin Falls
50 Mt Somers Peak

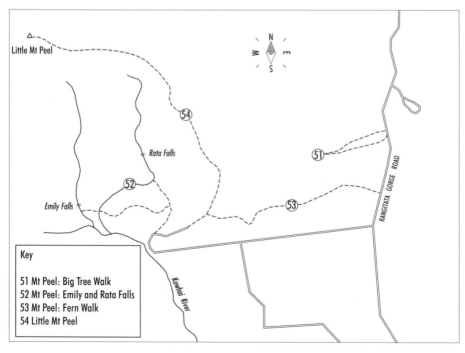

Key

51 Mt Peel: Big Tree Walk
52 Mt Peel: Emily and Rata Falls
53 Mt Peel: Fern Walk
54 Little Mt Peel

South Canterbury

South Canterbury is a quixotic mixed bag of walks and landscapes. Much of the early bush was cleared by settlers and the plains are now relentlessly rural, but here and there are some attractive bush reserves, such as Mt Nimrod/Kaumira, or short gorges such as Pareora.

Yet in the forested foothills there is a concentration of superb walks such as Peel Forest and Mt Somers. Only about half the number of walking possibilities have been included in this book.

Timaru has been developing several urban walks around its perimeter, and two excellent short walks are included here.

46 Methven Walkway

GRADE 1 to 2

TIME 3–4 hours one way full walk, or one hour 30 minutes one way from Forest Road to Ashburton River/Hakatere.

ACCESS There are numerous access points along this walkway, but the formal start of the walkway is roughly 1 km along the Rakaia–Barkers Road at a line of pines and redwood trees.

TRACK NOTES

Walkers will find it easy to choose a section of the 12 km walkway that suits their available time, and a map is helpful to decide the best start point. Arguably the most attractive section is from Forest Road to the Ashburton River/Hakatere, about 5 km one way (two to two hours 30 minutes return).

From Rakaia–Barkers Road, the walkway travels through long rows of conifers and redwoods, crosses Gorge Road beside the racecourse and continues to the Rangitata Diversion Canal. This large irrigation canal provides excellent walking as it snakes over the flat Canterbury countryside.

All fences have stiles and there are regular signposts as the track crosses Mt Harding Road, Forest Road, Ledgerwoods Road and Dip Road. You'll have excellent views of Mt Hutt, Mt Winterslow and Mt Somers as the track reaches the Ashburton River Road, and continues a short distance to the braided Ashburton River/Hakatere.

ABOVE: One of the many stiles on the Methven Walkway (46).

POINTS OF INTEREST

- At Ashburton River/Hakatere, the Rangitata Diversion Canal emerges from a siphon which is one of the largest working siphons in New Zealand; a pipe in the ground that carries the canal water underneath the riverbed, avoiding the necessity of bridging. In the early days of gold mining in New Zealand, many thousands of water-races were built, and every time the race came to a gully or river, the miners either had to bridge it by an aqueduct (or fluming as it was known then), or construct a siphon. This is a rare modern working example.

47 Mt Somers: Blackburn Coal Mine

GRADE 2

TIME Two hours return.

ACCESS Mount Somers township is 100 km from Christchurch. From the township take Ashburton Gorge Road (to Erewhon) and after approximately 10 km turn down a signposted gravel side-road for 3.5 km to the Coalminers Flat picnic area. This is a large, grassy and sheltered picnic area and campsite, with information boards and toilets provided.

TRACK NOTES

A pleasant hike through beech forest and up to the site of an interesting abandoned coal mine. Older children would enjoy this walk.

The first part of this walk leaves Coalminers Flat carpark and follows the main Mt Somers walkway (or Miners Track) alongside Woolshed Creek through black and silver beech trees. The track then picks up the old jig road to the foot of the jig railway incline.

The Mt Somers walkway zig-zags up the sharp jig incline to the bare bleached site of the Blackburn Coal Mine. A reconstructed mine entrance has been built, where you can learn about Gutsers and Banjo's.

POINTS OF INTEREST

- In 1864 the first coalfield was opened in the Woolshed Creek area, and in 1908 a tramway was built which, when completed, went from this mine to Mount Somers village. The tramway was to join the newly completed main trunk railway line in 1887. The Blackburn Coal Mine started life in 1928 but became uneconomic during the Depression and was closed. The mine resumed production in fits and starts although the coal was always poor quality and several underground fires closed the mine permanently in 1960.

- Four-tonne hoppers full of coal would plummet down from the mine, and by means of a self-acting pulley, the empty hoppers would be hauled up again. A few hoppers invariably ran off the rails and there is a good example of a mangled hopper at the foot of this incline.

48 Mt Somers: Woolshed Creek canyon

GRADE 3

TIME 4–5 hours return (or more if you spend time exploring the canyon area).

ACCESS As for Blackburn Coal Mine (47).

TRACK NOTES

This is a longer walk, following the same route to the Blackburn Coal Mine but continuing on to the top of Woolshed Creek canyon and the hut.

Beyond the mine site, a well poled track sidles over tussock gullies along the edge of Woolshed Creek Valley, then gradually climbs to Trig R. This is a splendid viewpoint.

The poled route nimbly descends past a rocky lookout and drops to the gouged and twisted canyon at the head of Woolshed Creek. The track fords the upper stream and leads directly to a former musterer's hut.

A poled side-track goes from the hut downstream into the top Woolshed Creek canyon, and the track zig-zags neatly under and around bluffs, dropping right into the base of the roaring canyon itself. A worthwhile side-trip (20 minutes).

POINTS OF INTEREST

- From Trig R you can see the Southern Alps and the peak of Mt Arrowsmith (3000 m), and beyond that, the distant headwaters of the Rangitata River — the mythical land of Erewhon that Samuel Butler made famous in his fictional satire. Butler's book title is an anagram of 'nowhere' (rather than, as is popularly believed, 'nowhere' spelled backwards).
- The headwaters of both Woolshed and Morgan creeks have a fascinating array of rock outcrops, water caves, waterfalls and deep crystal pools.
- Woolshed Creek Hut is a former station musterer's hut that has been extended to accommodate 18 people, and is equipped with a wood stove. This hut may be extended in the future as the Mt Somers walkway is a popular tramping route. There is also a unique sauna hut further up the valley (ten minutes).

49 Mt Somers: Sharplin Falls

GRADE 2

TIME One hour to one hour 30 minutes return to Sharplin Falls (including High Level Track), one hour 30 minutes to two hours return to Duke Knob and Ridge Track.

ACCESS Mount Somers township is situated 100 km from Christchurch, so to access Sharplin Falls turn right at Mt Somers and follow SH 72 some 7 km to Staveley, then follow signs for 3 km to Bowyers Stream carpark. Information signs, a shelter and toilets are found here.

TRACK NOTES

This is a sheltered and attractive area, and is a walk very suitable for families. Be warned that wasps can be a problem in late summer.

From the shelter and toilet at the carpark, cross the footbridge and follow the track upriver. The track to the falls is signposted, and wanders among beech forest beside the river, with one brief section of river boulders to pass.

The track then passes the boulder cascade of the Goldsmith Rapids, climbs along the impressive verandah bolted into the rock walls, before you finally get to the falls themselves that roar 10 m down a mossy, rock-strewn face.

There is an alternative, High Level Track (easy and well graded), that you can take back from the falls.

POINTS OF INTEREST

- Geologically, Mt Somers is an old volcanic rhyolite dome, quite distinctive from the greywacke that makes up most of South Canterbury and the Southern Alps, and Duke Knob is a characteristic outcrop. The forest is a mixture of mountain and black beech with a few scattered southern rata. Rata is sometimes called the 'Christmas Tree' because it flowers in December, though the brilliant red that attracts the korimako (bellbird) comes not from the petals, but from the circle of red stamens. There are also some totara, matai and kahikatea trees in this area. Typcial understorey plants include makomako (wineberry), papaumu (broadleaf), putaputaweta (marbleleaf) and horoeka (lancewood).
- Another walk option is to climb Duke Knob; follow Mt Somers walkway to the track junction, and continue on as it climbs steeply to the rhyolite rock peak of Duke Knob, which gives an excellent lookout over the upper valley of Bowyers Stream and Mt Somers.

- Black beech often has a sooty looking fungus growing on its trunk, which grows on the secretions of a scale insect feeding on sap under the bark. The tiny white 'anal tube' threads of the insect are visible, as are the sweet-tasting drops dangling at the end. Honey-eaters like tui, korimako (bellbird) and silvereye enjoy this bounty — as do the bees, who gather the secretions and turn it into what we call honey-dew. At certain times of the year the heady scent of honey-dew permeates the forest.

50 Mt Somers Peak

GRADE 4
TIME 6–8 hours return (a full day).
ACCESS As for Blackburn Coal Mine (47).
TRACK NOTES
Mt Somers is an accessible mountain for fit walkers, but the route along the tops is exposed and requires good weather. *You need to be well equipped and have a reliable map.* There is no marked or poled route to the summit, so in misty and foggy conditions it is very easy to get lost on the rolling and featureless tussock plateau. The peak is snow-covered in winter and the view from the top is one of the best in Canterbury.

From Coalminers Flat carpark, cross Woolshed Creek to the Nature Walk and follow this for ten minutes to a track junction. Turn up the signposted Tri Falls Stream Track. This track climbs quickly through beech forest, then up an open tussock and gravel spur, finally zig-zagging up a steep spur to the rim of the plateau.

You can continue along this track for a while on the gentle tussock slopes, but at some point you should check your map, take aim at any convenient spur and leave the track. You cannot see the summit yet.

Off-track travel is usually easy on the tussock spurs and as you climb the summit comes into view, but it is always further than it looks. All told, it is a 1000 m climb from Coalminers Flat. An odd sort of millennium monument sits on the summit.

From the summit of Mt Somers, the high peak of Aoraki/Mt Cook (3754 m) looks dramatically close, and inland you can see the peaks of Arrowsmith (2795 m) and D'Archiac (2865 m). To the north is the skifield at Mt Hutt and beyond that the Port Hills of Christchurch.

ABOVE: The seat and cairn atop Mt Somers (50).

51 Peel Forest: Big Tree Walk

GRADE 1

TIME 40 minutes return circuit.

ACCESS Roughly 15 km before Geraldine on SH 72, drive 12 km past the Peel Forest Visitor Centre to either Blandswood Road or Te Wanahu Flat (where there is a shelter and toilet). Peel Forest store and tearooms have all your supplies, and sell tickets to the attractive camping ground.

TRACK NOTES

This is a short walk on a gravelled path to an impressive totara. Good for a family stroll and usually busy with a healthy chorus of birds including the songs of riroriro (grey warbler), korimako (bellbird) and rifleman.

The track starts from beside the shelter at Te Wanahu Flat and meanders through tall forest, crossing a slight ridge and meeting the return track junction. A short distance further on is the massive 1000 year old totara that has a circumference of nine metres!

You can return on an alternative track to Te Wanahau Flat.

POINTS OF INTEREST

- Another big tree walk is the Dennistoun Bush Walk, which leads underneath stately kahikatea and matai to another massive totara. These trees are all podocarps or native conifers, and are descended from a lineage going back a hundred million years.
- Other walks on this side of Peel Forest include Allan's Track (two hours return), Acland Falls (one hour return) and Kahikatea Walk (one hour return).

52 Peel Forest: Emily Falls and Rata Falls Circuit

GRADE 2

TIME Two hour circuit to both waterfalls.

ACCESS As for Big Tree Walk (51).

TRACK NOTES

An interesting and varied circuit to two waterfalls, with a good chance of wet feet at some point. The river crossings are not hard (assuming it has not rained) and would suit children from eight years old.

From the small carpark at Blandswood Road, you need to walk back along the road a short distance to the signposted start of the track to Emily Falls. The track quickly reaches a seat and track junction with the Rata Falls track.

Take the Emily Falls track as it wanders down through the forest, crosses a stream and sidles around to another stream and the pretty Emily Falls. Retrace your steps to the first stream. A signpost indicates the route upriver.

There are about 45 stream crossings from the Emily Falls Track to the Rata Falls Track, then another ten stream crossings to Rata Falls itself. On your return, pick up the Rata Falls Track to complete the circuit.

POINTS OF INTEREST

- The jewelled gecko is present at Peel Forest, varying in colour from bright green to a grey-brown, with whitish stripes or diamond shaped markings on its back. The jewelled gecko is 150 mm long, and like most geckos it feeds mostly on insects and larvae. Geckos and skinks are all part of the lizard family, and nearly 40 species are known to exist in New Zealand, nearly all of them endemic (found only here). Geckos give birth to their young live and usually undergo a partial hibernation during cooler months.

ABOVE: Waterfall at the cool chasm of Rata Falls (52).

ABOVE: Fern Walk (53) on the Peel Forest trail.

53 Peel Forest: Fern Walk

GRADE 2
TIME 2–3 hours return.
ACCESS As for Big Tree Walk (51).
TRACK NOTES
A track through luxuriant fern and fuchsia forest, most suited to those interested in plants.

The track starts from the road just before Te Wanahu Flat and follows along quite close to the forest margin. There is a side-junction to Allan's Track here, and further on Fred's Seat provides a welcome rest spot.

The Fern Walk finishes on the main track to Deer Spur, only a short distance from the Blandswood Road carpark.

POINTS OF INTEREST
- Peel Forest is the best and virtually last remaining podocarp forest in South Canterbury. Botanically, it contains a huge variety of plant species from the forest floor to the alpine tops. For a temperate country, New Zealand is well-endowed with ferns and has 165 species, of which 78 are endemic. Peel Forest has 68 species of ferns in this tiny 700 ha remnant forest, which is more fern bio-diversity than the whole of Britain's 25 million hectares.

54 Little Mt Peel

GRADE 4
TIME 5–7 hours return.
ACCESS As for Big Tree Walk (51).
TRACK NOTES
A well marked, wonderful (and hard) daywalk. The views are superb, but take care as Little Mt Peel is exposed and gets plenty of snow in winter.

From the Blandswood Road carpark, the Deer Spur track passes the junction with Fern Walk (53) and climbs steadily through a mixed forest of fuchsia and broadleaf.

Occasional views of the plains are had as the track passes the junction with Allan's Track and some southern rata. The track enters the upper-alpine shrub-belt of turpentine, flax and dracophyllums beside the alpine tarn. This is a good turn-around point for people who do not fancy the entire climb.

ABOVE: The footbridge which straddles Saltwater Creek (55).

Now the track winds up the spur onto the tussock slopes, and there are extensive boardwalks higher up. The last 150 m is an even steeper climb to the sharp small top of Little Mt Peel. There is a beacon on top and a shelter 20 m below, which is enclosed with seats and a rainwater tank.

POINTS OF INTEREST

- As you climb Deer Spur the changes in plants and habitat are dramatic, starting with a fuchsia and fern forest in the lowland, then a layer of southern rata (look out for the crimson flowers at Christmas time). There are also some fine specimens of Spaniard (aciphylla) here, and their razor-sharp, flowering stalks often reach over a metre tall. Then, just 20 minutes above the tarn, is the harsh open alpine grassland of tussock and celmesias.

55 Saltwater Creek

GRADE 1

TIME One hour to one hour 30 minutes return.

ACCESS From SH 1 in Timaru take High Street, then South Street to a large carpark beside the Caledonian Grounds.

TRACK NOTES

A pleasant, urban/rural stroll with good coastal scenery. Good for families up to the footbridge, with a return along the beach.

From the carpark, cross the outlet (usually it is sanded up), and follow the poles through the scruffy scrub country on the beach. You may want to take the beach route itself. After 20 minutes, the track reaches a massive footbridge, and by following the stop-bank up the river you wander along the lagoon. On a fine day may see Aoraki/Mt Cook.

After you reach SH 1, you can either return the same way or cross the roadbridge and return via the Otipua Wetland, on the opposite bank of Saltwater Creek. Still being developed, the wetland area is already attracting many birds, and the track makes a pleasant circuit around the lake. A branch track continues down the south bank of the Saltwater Creek to the coast to rejoin the main Saltwater Track.

56 Dashing Rocks

GRADE 1

TIME One hour return from Virtue Avenue carpark, 30 minutes return from Pacific Street.

ACCESS From north Timaru, turn off from SH 1 onto Waimataitai Road, then drive on to Westcott Street and then Pacific Street to the track signposts.

TRACK NOTES

A surprisingly attractive urban walk along Timaru's northern coastline and around to the sea-arch and rock lava flows at the aptly named Dashing Rocks. From the Virtue Street carpark, follow the good track over the Benvenue Cliffs onto the grassy reserve that backs Waimataitai Bay. Walk up Richmond Street, then turn left along Climie Terrace to join the headland track. The track passes through pine trees and around the meatworks to a dramatic lookout over Dashing Rocks. If you continue a short distance around the broadland you can scramble onto the rocks

ABOVE: Day walkers at low tide, Dashing Rocks (56).

themselves and through the archway. **Note:** This should only be done at low tide and with a flat sea running. This was once a popular Maori fishing spot, but it can get rough and its name is well-earned.

The walkway continues down to the pretty bay, then crosses over rural land directly to Pacific Street. Follow Westcott Street onto Richmond Street and retrace your steps back to the carpark. There is also the option of walking over the footbridge at Benvenue Cliff and across the railway line to look at the lighthouse, built in 1878.

POINTS OF INTEREST

- In 1882, Benvenue Cliff was the site where two sailing ships, the *Benvenue* and *City of Perth*, were wrecked with the loss of nine lives.

57 Pareora River Walkway

GRADE 1 to 2

TIME One hour return.

ACCESS *You will need a good road-map to find this walk.* From south of Timaru (just over the Saltwater Creek), take Beaconsfield Road and turn left into Holme Station Road which quickly meets Pareora River Road. Follow this up Pareora River to the junction with Evans Crossing Road, and follow this next road a short distance to the ford and signpost on the far side. The Pareora River Walkway is situated roughly 20 km from Timaru.

TRACK NOTES

Although much of the original Pareora River Walkway is overgrown or has been closed down, the remaining section is delightful and leads to superb swimming holes beside to the old Pareora Dam. Great for a family outing.

From Evans Crossing Road follow the regularly spaced signposts across paddocks, as the track goes around the inner curve of the river. After 20 minutes some interesting rock formations begin to appear in the river, making an ideal picnic area.

The walk then picks up the remains of the historic water-race as it goes deeper into the little gorge, and swings around a tight bend in the river, shortly reaching the beautiful dam site. There is a huge swimming hole downstream of the waterfall, and another one above it. The walkway originally continued beyond here but is now overgrown and the marker posts have been removed.

ABOVE: Looking over the top of the old dam at Pareora River (57).

POINTS OF INTEREST
- The water-race was constructed in 1873 to supply Timaru city with a reliable source of water. Such was the importance of the event for the townspeople that the starting date for construction (5 March) was declared a public holiday and 200 people arrived at the Pareora River for the inauguration ceremony. However, the scheme was plagued with slips blocking the race, as well as with pollution. The intake dam was built in 1880 but problems persisted, and in 1939 the water-race was eventually replaced with a pipeline from the upper Pareora Gorge.

58 Nimrod Scenic Reserve

GRADE 3

TIME Three hours return via main track, or 15 minutes return for the intake walk.

ACCESS From SH 1 take the Pareora River Road to Craigmore Valley Road and Middle Yards Road. Turn north along Back Line Road to the signposted entrance to the reserve.

TRACK NOTES

A secluded bush reserve with a reasonably demanding walking track circuit to a waterfall. An attractive camping ground, set in the bush, is found at the start of the walk.

Cross the footbridge beside the camping area, as the track twists through fuchsia forest then begins a steep climb uphill to a bush saddle. There is a short sidetrack to a rocky knoll and lookout, otherwise continue on the main trail as it sidles in and out of gullies.

The track passes another rock lookout and then descends to Nimrod Stream. The pretty falls are just a short scramble upstream.

There is another steep climb from the streambed through bush and then tussock slopes to the high point (670 m), with some good views. The track continues steadily down the bush ridge and then back to the camping and picnic area.

POINTS OF INTEREST
- The forest is a mix of broadleaf, tarata (lemonwood) and fuchsia, with mahoe (whiteywood) on the higher slopes. There are some big matai and kahikatea remaining in places.
- The camping area is small, sheltered and attractive, and suited for families on a weekend out of town.

Aoraki/Mt Cook and Mackenzie Country

Mackenzie Country is a unique New Zealand landscape: raw, open, full of light. This tussock wilderness is a world away from the organised patchwork quilt of Canterbury, yet is separated from it by only one low pass. Burkes Pass was one of the routes that Maori took for seasonal food-gathering, and it later became the 'dray highway' in the 1850s as the first pioneer settlers moved into this harsh landscape.

Many of these settlers were of Scottish origin, and it is said that in 1858 there were more Gaelic speakers in the Mackenzie Country than English. James McKenzie was one of these, and his attempt to steal sheep and take them over a secret pass into the Mackenzie Basin in 1855 made him more notorious than he could ever have imagined. After two (or three) escapes from Lyttelton gaol, he was pardoned on the grounds that the trial was conducted in English and that McKenzie might not have understood it.

Lake Tekapo has several good walkways, and two of them have been included here. At Mount Cook village there are many great short walks, but it pays to pick your weather. The nor'wester that howls across the Mackenzie Country is famous for spoiling a few mountaineers' dreams.

59 Mt John: Ascent and Hilltop Circuit

GRADE 3

TIME Two hours climb and circuit.

ACCESS From Lake Tekapo township, take the road to the lakeside motor camp and continue to the carpark just before the ice-skating rink.

TRACK NOTES

Mt John offers a wonderful panorama of Lake Tekapo and the surrounding Mackenzie Country.

From the carpark beside the ice-skating rink, the track climbs steadily through the larch forest and reaches a junction with a loop track that circles the summit. There are seats here, and even here the views are good.

If you are walking the full circuit, take the track on the Lake Tekapo side and climb up to the rocky lookout where the views are even better. Mt John is surprisingly flat on top, and on occasion Himalayan chukor (an introduced game bird) can be spotted on the top slopes.

ABOVE: Marker poles line the pathway across the top of Mt John (59).

Continue on the Hilltop Circuit Track (pass the junction with the longer track option) as it winds around the hill, with wonderful views of Lake Tekapo and Lake Alexandrina, and return to the junction back down the hill to the lakeside carpark.

POINTS OF INTEREST

- For a longer circuit walk, take the Hilltop and Lake Circuit Track as it descends a long, easy spur for some 2 km to where the track drops sharply to Lake Tekapo itself. Staying 50 m above the lake, the track sidles around the base of Mt John and returns to the ice-skating rink and carpark. Add another hour to the total time if you are taking this longer track.

- You cannot climb to the actual top of Mt John (1031 m) because it is occupied by the astronomical observatory run by the University of Canterbury. Mt John was identified as one of the best sites in New Zealand for an observatory, because of its high percentage of clear nights and low light pollution. For many years, there used to be a controversial satellite-tracking station here, but that has now gone. Instead, in 1986, the university installed the reflecting McLellan telescope — New Zealand's largest, with an aperture of one metre. There are also two smaller reflecting telescopes of 61 cm aperture each.

- The Church of the Good Shepherd sits on a peninsula that juts into the sheer blue of Lake Tekapo – this must be one of the most photographed buildings in New Zealand. The foundation stone was laid by the Duke of Gloucester in January 1935 and the church was completed eight months later. It was designed by the architect R.S.D. Harman and is a memorial to high country settlers and shepherds. The church houses a book in which the early history of the district has been handwritten.

- The famous dog statue is in memory of all high country mustering dogs 'without the help of which the grazing of the mountainous country would be impossible'. The statue was cast in bronze by local artist Miss Elliott. Possibly New Zealand's first sheep-dog trials were held in the Mackenzie Basin at Haldon Station in 1869.

60 Tekapo Walkway: Lake George Scott Loop

GRADE 3

TIME One hour 30 minutes to two hours return.

ACCESS The walkway starts on SH 8 near Lake Tekapo beside the fire station and mapboard.

ABOVE: Lupins by the lake along Tekapo Walkway (60).

TRACK NOTES

An interesting walk that explores behind Lake Tekapo along the Tekapo River and gives excellent views of the mountains and township.

The track initially climbs steeply, following a fenceline onto a high river terrace which is typical of this area. There are good views of the mountains and the silent Tekapo River. The track elegantly descends into larch and conifer forest (past a track junction) onto a lower terrace, then follows the Tekapo River around to Lake George Scott. This lake was formed behind the Tekapo A dam.

The track has been altered here, and now continues along the road about half a kilometre to the prominent house, where a marker pole indicates the track up a fenceline back to the track junction.

POINTS OF INTEREST

- Construction began on Tekapo A power station in 1938 and the powerhouse and dam were completed by 1953. The lake was raised by a 61 m reinforced concrete dam, with a spillway for excess water. The water from the lake is taken by a 1.6 km tunnel to a 48-m-diameter surge tank, and then into the powerhouse itself. The tunnel was built through a ridge of unstable glacial moraine and required a new technique in its construction that involved the use of 'shields' – these were open-ended cylinders that were pushed into the moraine by hydraulic jacks; the spoil was then removed and a concrete lining put in place. The powerhouse contains a single generator of 25 MW (megawatt), with a Tampella turbine. The station is remotely operated entirely by the Twizel Control Centre.

- Russell lupins are believed to have been first introduced to the Mackenzie area at Dalrachney Station in the Lindis Pass in the 1930s. However, in 1952 the seed was sewn by Connie Scott and her son David of Godley Peaks Station, along road verges in the Burkes Pass and Lake Tekapo area. Lupins were later sewn by other people at the Hermitage at Aoraki/Mt Cook, with a consequent spectacular flowering in late spring. Sheep also like the Russell lupins, so the plants do not get far beyond the roadside fences.

61 Hooker Valley

GRADE 2 to 3

TIME 3–4 hours return to ice lake.

ACCESS From SH 80, turn off just before the Mount Cook village and go to the large carpark and camping area under White Horse Hill. Picnic tables and toilets are found here.

TRACK NOTES

The Hooker Valley is a fine walk into the heart of Aoraki/Mount Cook National Park, with gorges, glaciers, lakes and (in season) the Mount Cook lily to see.

The track starts from the White Horse camping area and passes the original site of the Hermitage and an alpine memorial. The track zig-zags down to the first swingbridge across the milky-blue Hooker River.

Good views continue up-valley past the Mueller Glacier terminal lake, and the track cuts along a gorge with another spectacular swingbridge. After the bridge, the track runs around to the Stocking Stream shelter and toilet.

After a flat section with some boardwalks, the track goes over a slight rise and you reach the 'ice lake' or terminal lake of the Hooker Glacier.

POINTS OF INTEREST

- The Mount Cook lily (*Ranunculus lyalli*) is really the world's largest buttercup. Other interesting plants to see include the spikey matagouri shrub, the sharp spandiard and the tiny New Zealand edelweiss.
- Hooker was named by Julius von Haast after William Hooker, an English botanist and father of Joseph Hooker. Mt Cook was named of course

ABOVE: Ice lake at the end of the Hooker Valley walk (61).

after the explorer Captain James Cook, and the five highest peaks in New Zealand are called 'The Navigators' because each is named after a famous captain: Cook, Tasman, La Perouse, Dampier and Elie de Beaumont.

- The Maori name for the mountain is Aoraki (or, in many North Island tribal dialects, Aorangi), which is translated by some as 'cloud piercer'.

Sealey Tarns

This area is mainly suited to the experienced, fit walker, as the track is ruthlessly steep with a series of unending steps. The views are excellent on a fine day with a chance to photograph Aoraki/Mt Cook's reflection in the tarns.

From the junction with the Kea Point Track, the track to Sealey Tarns starts easily enough, climbing steadily to a small boulder scree where orange triangles point you in the right direction. The next 300 m is almost vertical! The track zig-zags up steps and occasionally scrambles over rock slabs and hillsides covered with alpine scrub. Just when you think that the climbing will never end, the track softens a mite, then sides into tussocks and reaches the graceful oasis of the two tarns.

You might feel relieved you are not continuing up to Mueller Hut, another 400 m further still.

62 Kea Point and Sealey Tarns

GRADE 1 to 3

TIME One hour return to Kea Point from White Horse camping area, one hour 30 minutes return from Hermitage Hotel, or two to three hours return to Sealey Tarns and White Horse camping area.

ACCESS As for Hooker Valley (61).

TRACK NOTES

Kea Point is a popular short walk with superb alpine views, and is a chance to see (or at least hear) the kea (mountain parrot). The karearea (New Zealand falcon) can often be seen and heard here also.

From the White Horse shelter the well graded track winds through groves of alpine toatoa and matagouri, and meets a junction with the Hermitage Track. The path from here turns into a quiet back-valley and passes the junction to the Sealey Tarns Track. Kea Point is another 15 minutes further and it is worth going onto the spectacular platform lookout, with views over the unstable moraine walls and the glacier-fed lake.

63 Red Tarn

GRADE 2 to 3

TIME Two hours to two hours 30 minutes return.

ACCESS Start from the public shelter on the Mount Cook village loop road, not far from the shop and beside Governors Bush. Toilets and information panels are found here.

TRACK NOTES

The Red Tarns are a refuge from the tourist hubbub of Mount Cook village, offering good views back over the village.

At the public shelter, signs direct you along a gravelled path beside a bubbling creek, then out of the village to a long footbridge over the Black Birch Stream. The track then starts to climb steeply through the alpine scrub of flax, turpentine and totara. It crosses occasional gullies on its way to the rim of the basin — all told a 500 m climb to the tarns.

POINTS OF INTEREST

- There is a seat and plane table beside the tarn, which gets the name Red Tarn (rather prosaically) from the red pond weed that grows in it. On a still, sharp day you can see a perfect reflection of Aoraki/Mt Cook in the tarnp.